I0210596

UNFILTERED
AND
UNAPOLOGETIC

UNFILTERED
AND
UNAPOLOGETIC

A WOMAN'S GUIDE
TO LIVE, LOVE, AND LEAD
WITH BOLDNESS

JUDY MCCUTCHEON

Advantage | Books

Copyright © 2025 by Judy McCutcheon.

All rights reserved. No part of this book may be used or reproduced in any manner whatsoever without prior written consent of the author, except as provided by the United States of America copyright law.

Published by Advantage Books, Charleston, South Carolina.
An imprint of Advantage Media.

ADVANTAGE is a registered trademark, and the Advantage colophon is a trademark of Advantage Media Group, Inc.

Printed in the United States of America.

10 9 8 7 6 5 4 3 2 1

ISBN: 979-8-89188-147-1 (Paperback)
ISBN: 979-8-89188-148-8 (eBook)

Library of Congress Control Number: 2025902362

Cover design by Matthew Morse.
Layout design by Ruthie Wood.

This publication is designed to provide accurate and authoritative information in regard to the subject matter covered. It is sold with the understanding that the publisher is not engaged in rendering legal, accounting, or other professional services. If legal advice or other expert assistance is required, the services of a competent professional person should be sought.

Advantage Books is an imprint of Advantage Media Group. Advantage Media helps busy entrepreneurs, CEOs, and leaders write and publish a book to grow their business and become the authority in their field. Advantage authors comprise an exclusive community of industry professionals, idea-makers, and thought leaders. For more information go to **advantagemedia.com**.

To my mom and daughters.

CONTENTS

INTRODUCTION
Starting the Conversation

This book is written solely with you in mind. It's meant to help you start that difficult conversation with yourself. You know, the one so many of us avoid at all costs: the conversation surrounding ourselves, our happiness, and whether we ever thought about what we wanted before we started handing out pieces of ourselves to the rest of the world.

We are an afterthought. Like it or not, the truth is, it's how many of us treat ourselves.

We schedule our days so full that we are constantly on the go, tired, beaten down, and within an inch of our lives, ensuring we're busy doing everything for everyone else, pleasing everyone else—everyone but ourselves. What is this obsession that we have with martyrdom? It's almost as if, in self-sacrifice, we have finally found that elusive orgasm. The one we have only heard described but have never gotten to experience for ourselves. Maybe in some sick, masochistic way, we have finally found that gratification we so desperately desired, but at what cost?

I've done that shit for years, putting myself last, making sure everyone else was satisfied, never mind the fact I was left wanting. I was stuck in a vicious cycle where I tended to everyone and everything but myself.

We surround ourselves with people we think we can trust, but sometimes, the people we trust most prove our judgment wrong. No matter how much we want to believe the best about people, the truth is that some people operate out of selfishness, insecurity, or even out of a desire to use another's success to catapult their own agenda, career, or finances forward, regardless of the cost to others.

This is one reason it is so important to, first and foremost, *always* focus on your relationship with yourself so you are able to discern and determine what the best course of action is for you and the trajectory of your life, no matter what others might think.

"Judy, you can't fix people; it is not your job to fix them," a friend once told me. And you know what? She's right. I'm going to tell you the same thing she told me: *It is not your job to fix others.* Stop trying to be a people pleaser—instead, focus on the one thing you actually have control over.

UNFILTERED:

Focus on fixing the only person you can fix—YOU.

I watched an interview with Oprah Winfrey where she explained that, before she agrees to do a show or an interview, she asks herself what the purpose is. She must have a frame or context that makes sense, or she won't do it.

The context or frame for me writing this book is to get you thinking intentionally about your life and purpose. Why are you here? Why do you do the things you do? Why are you still in that bad relationship? Why are you holding out for material gain at the expense of your happiness?

Why are your fears and self-doubts still holding you back?

This book's purpose is to get you to change the conversations you have with yourself, about yourself. It is designed to help you stop making excuses and get up and take charge of you.

My conversations with myself helped me to become the person I am today. They have helped me turn my life around. I have been able to accomplish this by quitting all the negative self-talk I was engaging in, by affirming myself with each new step, and by making self-love my mantra.

My hope is that you can identify with what is written on these pages and use it to propel you into being the greatest *you* ever.

No limits. No holding back. You are going to give yourself 110 percent of your attention because, for too long, you have been giving everyone else 99 percent, and it has left your cup empty. It is time for you to refill your reservoirs and nurture your water supply so you can grow, thrive, and treat yourself the way you deserve to be treated.

You don't need a university degree. You don't need to be slim. You don't need to be Black or White, or any other color for that matter. You just need your badass self, a passion for life, and the persistence to carry on even when things get hard.

You need to live unfiltered and unapologetic.

ARE YOU TIRED YET?

I have had so many failures and disappointments in my life that I don't even know which of them have led me to success. I suppose it is the combination of them all to some degree—the lessons learned from losses and the determination to win after defeat. Even as I write these words, I am battling with a major disappointment, and I am asking myself some soul-searching questions.

UNAPOLOGETIC:

One of the best weapons in our arsenal is self-reflection. You won't win every battle because sometimes the lesson of the loss will bring you more value, but it is still important to be able to think through things rationally and reevaluate what has occurred.

What could we have improved upon that might have changed an outcome? Maybe it was the way we delivered information, maybe it was a reaction to information that was given to us, or maybe we handled everything to the best of our ability but learned that the environment didn't suit us or that we clashed with a particular personality type.

I got to the point in life where I was sick and tired of being a fool, sick and tired of doubting myself, and sick and tired of allowing my fears to paralyze me. I was sick and tired of telling myself that I was not good enough—I just got sick and tired of not living my best life. I knew there was more out there than this. That *more* was the reason I left my marriage and stopped settling for less than what I deserved. Yet, here I was, once again giving myself less than I deserved.

My starting point for doing things differently was my internal dialogue. I was my worst critic. According to me, I had no noteworthy attributes. I was a big ole failure, and that was that. I was in such a mental dump that I failed to realize all of my blessings. I wasn't in the space where I could recognize and appreciate my God-given gifts and talents so I could use them as a blessing to others.

I had to reverse the things I believed about myself and adjust my thinking so that my conversations could be different.

UNFILTERED:

If we want different in our lives, then we must think different, act different, be different.

A SINGLE THOUGHT

Everything starts with our thoughts and beliefs. What we see on the outside is just a manifestation of what is happening on the inside.

So many people are now talking about the law of attraction and manifesting what you desire. A lot of them want you to pay them to tell you how to do it, and nothing is wrong with that. You just have to know that success requires work. Your thinking must be in alignment and in harmony with the universal laws. What you think, what you desire, what you expect, and what you do must mesh.

It's not about what others think of you or expect you to be. I know I have simplified it, but it's to make you see that it's all about *your* thinking and *your* belief system—nothing more, nothing less. If you think you are the greatest at something, then your mind works to ensure that you become the greatest.

To change your life, you have got to change the way you think. Heck, Muhammad Ali had not yet won a single championship fight when he told the world he was the greatest, and that is exactly what he became in life. He knew it in his mind, had decided upon it and internalized it, and so he lived it.

Our mind is the most powerful tool we have, so we must let it work for us. We have two minds: the conscious and the unconscious mind. We communicate to the world through our conscious mind, and when it thinks correctly and is in alignment, we are able to harness our strengths, attracting all that is good and pure to ourselves and others. However, when our conscious mind is out of alignment, then our hell on earth shows up. We are in distress; we lack; we are governed by our limitations, and a bunch of other things that are not in harmony with what we want.

Now, our unconscious mind—that is where goodness is made. It is subjective and takes direction from the conscious mind. Whatever is fed to the unconscious mind is what is accepted. Because of this, we must train our conscious mind to give us the things we desire. We must coordinate these two minds to work in tandem with one another. The future we want is entirely within our control—I *dare* you to start now.

In the quest to better our lives, the starting point is ourselves. Your betterment is an inside job. What are you telling yourself about *you*? Oftentimes, many of the opinions we have about ourselves are not ours. Somebody, at some point in our lives, may have told us that we were a failure and would never amount to anything—and if this erroneous message has come from a parent, trusted family member, or someone else with a position of respect and authority, we often internalize it.

Of course, if Mommy or Daddy said it, then it must be true. So, we begin to think and act like failures to prove them right. I remember my humanities and social biology teacher told me that she almost fainted when she saw my final examination results. Even when you do well, there are those mentally inept adults who are hell-bent on destroying your little bit of hope.

I have news for you: Other people's opinions of you, even if they are your mother's, are none of your business. You are grown now; you are no longer that child you once were, and you must now allow that little girl to let go of past hurts and heal so that the beautiful woman you are can finally shine through.

This, my friends, is a difficult journey, even for the toughest badass. It is not a journey that I would advise you to take alone; I certainly didn't. I benefited tremendously from the assistance of both a therapist and a life coach.

If you can afford either or both, I encourage you to invest in such help. If you choose carefully, it will be money well spent. If, however, you are not currently financially able to hire a professional to walk with you on this journey of self-rediscovery, then there are plenty of books out there that can help you shift your perspective. You are reading one right now *wink*, but I also personally love *The Power of Now* by Eckhart Tolle.

Regardless, you must start by reversing your internal dialogue. Stop telling yourself that you are not good enough—know that you are more than enough as you are at this very moment. I tell my two girls all the time that they are more than enough.

For your own healing, you must acknowledge the little girl within. Acknowledge her hurts, her pains, her betrayals, and disappointments, and then give her permission to run free. I did it with an awesome fire release ceremony. I wrote a letter to myself, forgiving me for all the things I ever thought about myself that were bad or limiting. Everything I ever blamed myself for was in that letter. I brought the letter to a large bonfire, where I put it into the flames and stood in the heat as my life was cleansed. I let go of little Judy Jack so that this fabulous Judy Jack of today could shine through. It was ceremonial, and one of the most meaningful things I have ever done in my life.

There were other things on the horizon, too, that would help me get to where I am today. It begins with a crucial realization that is often forgotten.

A FEW THINGS TO REMEMBER

You are fearfully and wonderfully made. You must claim that right. Do not shrink from it. You were created to have a positive impact on this world, so find your gifts and use them to bless yourself as well as others. We all have talents; do not bury them! Invest them, sow them into good soil, and ensure you get a return on them.

Making peace with your past is a great way to safeguard your future. Learn to accept yourself—faults, bad habits, blemishes, and all. It is the only way you can truly see the areas that need development so that you can work on making yourself better today than you were yesterday.

A big part of that acceptance is love. You must learn to love yourself unconditionally. I believe that you are not capable of loving someone else if you don't first love yourself. You must experience that deep satisfaction and warmth when you close your eyes and wrap your arms around yourself before you can experience it with another human being.

To get yourself on the road, start to change the conversations you have with yourself.

HOW TO USE THIS BOOK

Again, the purpose of this book is to get that conversation going and then flowing. Each chapter will have lessons from my life that I hope will change your own, plus prompts at the end I call "A Conversation with Yourself" to change your mindset as you embark on the most significant relationship of all: the one you have with yourself. Reminders will appear along the way in special "unfiltered" and "unapologetic" prompts.

My hope is that you will read this book in its entirety, mark it up, highlight the lines that give you chills, underline the ones that really hit home, and share the stories and lessons with your girlfriends. Certain chapters will have deeper meaning, and you can mark them for a return visit when life twists or becomes more complicated. Friends, I've been there—and I want you to think of this book as a resource and a companion.

My dream is that you live an unfiltered life where you express yourself as wonderful, wise, one-of-a-kind *you*. Along the way, there will be doubters, for sure, but if you live unapologetically in your truth (while taking accountability, of course, along the way), then that is what I believe is a recipe for a fulfilled life.

I love this quote from Ashley Rickards: "The power you have is to be the best version of yourself you can be so that you can create a better world."

Let's do so together.

CHAPTER ONE
Unfiltered and Unapologetic

Be bold. Be brave. Be badass.

For years, I've signed off with this message. As the CEO of Go Blue Consulting, I've lived that passion daily, helping organizations empower leaders—particularly women—to reach their fully badass potential.

The actual word *badass* has many meanings for me, and I'm sure it does for you, too. I assure you that I'm talking about *badass* in the best possible sense of the word. We'll examine what it means to embody being a badass throughout the book, but for starters, a badass pursues whatever fascinates her and brings her to life, even if it requires taking a wild leap of faith. It means sometimes living with an absurd overconfidence in yourself.

That is the story of my life: taking chances and having faith in myself. Discovering my badass self—and letting her run the show—is how I got to where I am today. I work with some of the larger companies around the Caribbean and with many more institutions and private individuals to help them streamline processes, enhance productivity and engagement, retain top talent, and improve the bottom line. But I wasn't always a CEO. For me, my journey to badass began much earlier—growing up on the tiny island of Tobago.

If life is a numbers game, I was eight out of ten. Later, reaching a ten would mean hitting most of my life goals, but when I was younger, it was different. Then, it meant six brothers and three sisters. Most were already grown when I was a little girl, but five of us were lucky enough to live under the same roof with our mother. Her name is Molly, but we call her Mammy, and she was the first real badass in my life.

We lived in Tobago, in the twin-island Republic of Trinidad and Tobago. My home was a beautiful island in the Caribbean that had a vibrant culture, gorgeous beaches, and diverse vegetation. Growing up in a warm, tropical climate meant there were always fruit trees, which provided guava, mangoes, plums, and sugar cane—my favorites were the mangoes and plums.

The island always provided food to eat, which was lucky because my mother often struggled to put food on the table. She raised us alone, in one of the old apartment buildings that dot the island, and though I knew my father and would visit him, he had several children in Tobago, and most didn't live with him. My mother and father never lived together. He had three distinct families and a few children scattered here and there. I think he had fifteen in all. My mother had five kids with my father, and he proved to be less than helpful. Mammy was on her own in all the ways that counted. She was quite young and had hard decisions to make on a daily basis, so she had no other choice but to be a badass and step into the power position in the most exceptional way.

She worked almost around the clock, occupying her days with her job with the government before racing home to begin her second job, washing and ironing clothing, all while taking care of her children. My mother was also very civic-minded and belonged to several church and community groups; she even volunteered as the secretary for one of the major political parties in our district at that time. She spent every waking hour ensuring we were not only well cared for but well educated. She valued education and felt it was our ticket out of poverty. At that time, only the last five of us were able to attend high school, and I was fortunate enough to attend a private one. My mother was my everything in those days—the sole head of our household, singular wage earner, cook, therapist, and holder of her children's dreams.

We were rich in love, had great values, and had a stellar example to follow in Mammy. Money may have been tight, but Mammy reminded us that we had each other. She taught us that every single obstacle—and there are many when you live in survival mode—was just another opportunity filled with possibilities to win.

Of course, there were despairing moments. Circumstances conspired; life turned upside down. The paycheck didn't arrive. Rent was due. It was the end of the month. The fridge was empty and the cupboards were bare, so we knew there would be no food, but my older sister would announce it loud enough for the neighbors to hear. We grew up in a time when people looked out for each other, the neighbors would always help feed the kids around them, and there were always fruits available for us to eat.

I considered myself fortunate in those days—even lucky—and I still do, because there was always something good in each day, and Mammy taught us how to look for the good.

Back then, I was young, strong, healthy, and enterprising. As a kid, I didn't complain. I knew what there was and what there wasn't. There was no shame, no blame. My mother was trying her best. Even as a young girl, I had a few tricks up my worn sleeves in terms of intuition, moxie, and the ability to rise from rock bottom. Those traits would serve me well later in life, in marriage, in motherhood, and in eventually running Go Blue Consulting.

From my mother's example of being a badass, I developed the belief that if you win, it's a victory. If you fail, it's a lesson. The rest? Just blessings.

So, even now, I refuse to look at my childhood as lacking. The people who made up the fabric of our magical island supported my mother, and if a day was mean to her or distinctively tough, she pushed on.

Badass all the way.

My mother propelled me into being the greatest, most badass *me* I could be, and with this book, I hope to help you do the same. Like my mother showed me, when things get hard, all you need is a passion for life and the persistence to carry on. For us women, that can be a hard idea to wrap our minds around. We have been told there are *so* many things we *need* to be in order to "make it." We need more degrees, we need to be a certain weight, a certain race, etc., blah blah blah—*Stop! No!* All you *need* to be a badass, living the life of your dreams, is to be brave and to be bold. Like my mother, you can do anything you put your mind to, today, with exactly the things you have right now, exactly the way you are already.

Many women don't get to live their lives to the fullest. We want to be liked so badly that we don't know how to say no or set our own boundaries. We often consider ourselves an afterthought, allowing the other people in our orbit to take the lead. We keep ourselves so busy doing things for others that we risk giving up on our own hopes and dreams.

Yes, there is satisfaction in helping others, loving others, and putting others first, but following the path of others, never once choosing a path of your own, ultimately leads only to dead ends. I should know; I did it for years, putting myself last as I ensured that everyone got theirs, because at least *they* were satisfied. Never mind that I was left empty, wanting, lacking, and stuck in a vicious cycle of tending to others at the expense of my own needs, desires, and dreams.

You can do this professionally by working nonstop in ways that don't really get you ahead but do get you headaches and stuck in hard places. You can do this personally if you misjudge and surround yourself with people you think you can trust, whom you believe have your best interests at heart, only to be blind to the red flags until you realize too late that your judgment was wrong.

It's never too late to make some changes.

This book will serve as a guide on how to live fully as the badass you are in any of the various, all-important areas of your life, including family, work, important decisions, romantic encounters, child-raising, dream building, and giving back. I have designed the chapters so that the book can be read as a whole or in whatever order you need, depending on when you need a little extra inspiration or help to tackle a particular challenge you may be facing in your life. However you choose to read through these chapters, *Unfiltered and Unapologetic* is meant to help you with the difficult conversations you need to have with yourself—as I have had to do with myself at many turning points in my life—if you want to truly live and feel like a badass. These are the topics so many of us avoid at all costs: our happiness, our joy, our motivation, and the pieces of ourselves we give to family and hand out to the rest of the world. But don't worry; I will be by your side each step of the way, sharing stories from my own life and revealing the conversations I've had with myself over the years to remind myself of the badass I am.

You may not have lived a life that even remotely resembles mine, but if you've picked up this book and read this far already, then we have something cosmic in common—a passion for our own human potential. My story is your story is her story. It is my hope that you can identify with what is written on these pages and use my stories and life lessons to propel you into being the greatest *you* ever. If my years on this planet can somehow be a catalyst for you, if my life story can somehow help another person going through similar things, then writing this book will be not only worthwhile but will be a game changer for me, too.

So, no limits. No holding back. It's time to give yourself 110 percent of your attention because for too long you have been giving everyone else 99 percent. This book will help stoke your self-awareness, fanning flames of inspiration and disavowing doubt. When you feel empowered, you will thrive and fly.

Say it with me: "I vow to live full and out loud."

Be bold. Be brave. Be badass.

Now, let's go.

A CONVERSATION WITH YOURSELF

Stop telling yourself:

- I am not qualified or capable.

- My dreams are too big.

- I am messed up. (If you think you are, then you'd better get prayed up.)

Start telling yourself:

- I am enough exactly as I am.

- I come from strong, resilient ancestors.

- I am fearlessly badass.

What else can *you* stop and start telling yourself?

NOTES
FOR YOUR JOURNEY

CHAPTER TWO

Early Unfiltered Lessons

As a young girl, I dwelled with my family in a vibrant, small village in the Tobago countryside. My powerhouse mother, who weighed just about a hundred pounds, was the original badass. She had beautiful, long, dark, natural hair, plus a bright smile. She was known for a work ethic that was made of steel, often working ten hours a day before she did additional jobs for associations, including local political parties and women's unions. She even put on an annual sports event for the children in our village. I remember that she always worked two jobs to make sure we had a roof over our heads.

Our lives played out in a tiny, one-bedroom apartment on the bottom floor of someone's house. They still call them upstairs-and-downstairs houses. Our home didn't have running water, so we bathed and did dishes outside, used an outhouse, and had few material things. But still, I never once thought of us as poor. Maybe that was my first unapologetic move—an attitude of positivity ingrained by my mother and cemented by my own steely will. I was sure of one thing: We weren't coming from a place of lack. We were growing.

I didn't experience anything else other than what we had—and I was happy. I really had a joyous childhood because I was able to eat on most days. Gourmet? No. But it was filling. I had clothes, even though they were hand-me-downs. There was always laughter, fun, and love.

We were also a progressive house. We didn't have gender-based roles. Everyone had to pitch in because Mammy was busy earning the money. As for the rules, we had to be home at a certain hour, boy or girl. No one was tougher, smarter, or better at life. That was a win within a very traditional society—another way we were growing.

Through my mother's hard work and sacrifice, she was eventually able to build us a wooden, two-bedroom house. At one point, seven of us were living under one small roof, meaning that my mother had one of the bedrooms, and six of us children shared the other one. As children, we would fight with each other, which is what kids do, especially in such close quarters. Yet, if an outsider ever messed with one of us, they messed with *all* of us. We had each other's backs, no questions asked. The undeniable truth was that, as a unit, we were unbreakable.

STANDING UP FOR OTHERS

During my primary school days, I remember my sister Nelva getting beaten by the principal for something she did not do. Someone else did it and said it was her fault. Nelva got punished for this harmless prank, which meant corporal punishment, or "licks," as they called it back in those days. Basically, the adults would beat a kid with a belt in front of the entire school at assembly. How many licks the kid received depended upon the infraction. Looking back, I realize that some of the teachers suffered trauma in their lives that they didn't know how to process, so they took it out on the children. I will never forget the vengeance with which they would beat these kids, which just continued the cycle of pain.

On the day I had to watch my sister being beaten, I cussed out the principal. Good thing I was a fast runner and got out of there at record speed. I was so angry at the injustice of it all, and I cringed at how he had humiliated my sister. Corporal punishment is always cruel and unusual. After I left that school, I never spoke to that cruel man again.

It makes me angry to see someone being abused. I just don't see the need for that kind of behavior. And so, growing up, I often found myself speaking up and getting in the middle of altercations. In those days, we didn't call it bullying, but if someone was picking on another kid, I would step in because I hate a bully in any form. I couldn't fight with fists because I didn't know how, but I knew how to defend with my words. I had a lot of those because I was constantly reading and writing. That came in handy when I went into defense mode.

I've always felt it was necessary to be the voice for the voiceless, as I have a keen sense of justice. In my family, we still joke that if my mother had a few extra dollars, I would have become a lawyer.

UNAPOLOGETIC:

Speak up for those who can't speak for themselves. There is no need for anyone to take advantage of others. My speaking up was my first unfiltered move in life, but certainly not my last.

By the way, I don't remember *ever* getting licks in school.

A TICKET OUT OF POVERTY

All my brothers and sisters went to public school, but my mother chose to send me to a private Catholic school. It was expensive—$380 a term—and she sacrificed a lot to ensure I received a great education and a different experience. My mother also felt a private school might allow me to meet a different set of people from those in my village. The convent was in town, and we lived in the country. It was important to her that I meet people from different backgrounds. She had to make cuts that seemed impossible to make sure my early school fees were paid and we still had food, but again, Mammy knew the value of an education, telling us over and over, "Education is your ticket out of poverty."

Meanwhile, many of my mother's friends thought the idea of educating a girl in this way seemed absurd, which is often where some of our lightbulb moments come from in life. You find the seemingly most unreachable dream and then figure out a way to make it real. But at that age, at a private school and hanging out with those moneyed kids, I wasn't really applying myself. I was playing the fool and skipping classes, even though I knew my mother was sacrificing a lot for me to be there. I took my exams, and my mother didn't think I did well enough. It wasn't about intelligence but about application. She decided I needed to go to another private school, a Seventh-day Adventist school.

By that time, money was even tighter.

But Mammy wouldn't take no for an answer and even sought out my father for financial help. He didn't think I should go back to school at all, but my mother was adamant that I go back and explore different subjects from those I had pursued at the convent school. My father wasn't a rich man, but he was comfortable from his work as a tractor operator for the government.

"Don't you have some responsibility to your daughter?" Mammy demanded. Later, I would realize that I had gotten a lot of my drive and courage—my unfiltered core—from my mother. She just kept going. She never stopped when she had a goal. There was always another way to make it happen. She just got it done.

She ultimately got my father to agree to pay for my new private school education, but it still wasn't going to be easy.

My father did not (or could not) write a check for the entire school year, or even one semester. My life was on the installment plan, and there were many months that my father simply "forgot" to pay my school bill.

I refused to be discouraged. By this time, I was living with Miss Natalie, one of my teachers, who went to school with my brother and sister. This mentor saw a bright light in me, and we became close enough that she offered me a room in her house during the week to make the commute to school easier. For the first time in my life, I had my own bedroom and bathroom. The plan was that I'd go home on the weekends, but eventually, I didn't go back anymore. Miss Natalie was married to a chief engineer, and they lived in a lovely government house with four bedrooms. It might seem strange that she would offer me this lifeline, but she knew my plight, and the truth is that it was the norm in our community on the island to help each other out.

When tuition was due, I would wake up at four in the morning, and Miss Natalie would graciously drive me to my father's house on the other side of the island. She waited outside while I would walk in to find him eating breakfast and getting ready for work.

I was a collector for my own future.

"Daddy, I came to get my school fees," I would tell him.

I'm not sure if he was just rewarding effort, but he would pay. Month after month, it was the same early morning routine. It was all in the name of collecting my school fees, because a badass doesn't let obstacles get in her way. She finds the way out of them.

STARTING FROM THE BOTTOM

It's a good thing that I went the extra mile, literally. That private high school not only taught me worthwhile life skills that would jump-start my career, but it also introduced me to some of my earliest life helpers. Miss Natalie remained a mentor. Not only did I continue living with her, but we became quite close. Miss Natalie constantly reminded me that I had a bright future, telling me, "You can do it." Her words were gold to me.

It's funny how a twist of someone else's fate can change your life.

One day, Miss Natalie got a teaching job in Trinidad and asked me to move with her. So I did. I relocated with no job and no real plan, yet I decided I would go because I knew I wanted more from my life than what Tobago offered me at that time.

Trinidad was the larger and more populated of the two major islands of Trinidad and Tobago. The economy there was brighter, thanks to the flourishing natural gas industries that make Trinidad one of the top six exporters of liquefied natural gas in the world. Bag in hand, I moved to this oil-rich sister island with nothing but my dreams and youthful enthusiasm.

There are stories of people who cast their fates to a new place with $500 or even just $100 in their wallets, but that wasn't the case with me. *Please!* I had zero. Nothing. Not a dollar. I just had potential—and hope. I moved with one bag of clothes and promised to pay Miss Natalie back for the initial food and rent bills. We lived in a two-bedroom apartment, and we were fine—*ish*. She was making money while I hit the ground looking for work.

I was on my own at nineteen, trying to support myself—so I could (hopefully) not live hand-to-mouth—by working as many hours as possible to start my new life and repay Miss Natalie for her kindness.

UNFILTERED:

You must always remember where you came from and those who helped you along the way.

"Something will happen," I told myself. "Something *must* happen."

In the early days of job hunting, I got a job at Kentucky Fried Chicken. I had this great vision of being on fry duty. Instead, I was handed a mop.

Your goals are based on your level. At that time, my big goal was to make fries, but my bosses saw it differently. I left that job after three days, and not because I couldn't mop. I was just full of pride and had no humility. It was the exuberance of youth. This moment taught me I could make stupid decisions, but I could reflect and learn from those mistakes. What I learned was that being put on mop duty triggered my feelings of inadequacy and "not enoughness." I felt that management did not see me as someone of worth, and I thought that was why I was put on mopping duty.

I didn't recognize that mopping was all part of the training process.

The truth is that starting at the bottom often means a lower salary, longer shifts, and less appealing day-to-day tasks. You could hate that time of your life, or you could realize that it is also the beginning of life's journey. There is less required at the bottom, but it's still a badass move because you're there to learn without immediately taking on all that responsibility and stress.

It also gives you the cushion time to figure out where your strengths and weaknesses will fall. Use this time to learn the business and discover what interests you.

As we try to plant the foundation of our adult life, it's common to run face-first into self-esteem issues. It's usually an internal war where you wonder, *Don't they see me for who I am?*

The answer is that they do see you as having no experience and possibly nothing to bring to the party (yet). That's why they hand you the mop—an actual or metaphorical one. The mop can also be that coffee you're sent to fetch or the notes you take while others talk at the meeting.

I wish I could tell you that I mopped for a few months and learned my lessons. But the truth is that the young badass me decided to quit after only three days. *Oh well*, I thought. *I'll get another job that's better than fast food.*

I did find another place of employment, working in an office for a business. I did this for only a short time before I realized that my boss was scamming money from innocent people. You'll hear that story in the next chapter, but suffice to say that it was illegal and certainly not moral. As broke as I was in those days, I just couldn't be a part of it, even in a small way, because I would not compromise my convictions.

UNAPOLOGETIC:

Your good name and convictions are your moral center. The most badass move of all is to walk away when either is compromised. Conducting yourself from this higher level will never be the wrong decision.

At nineteen, I didn't know what I didn't know. This was a unique time to explore, experiment, and try life on. I was proud of myself for not compromising my integrity for money. I knew it then, and I know it with a real truth now: it's never going to be worth it.

IF YOU DON'T ASK, IT WON'T HAPPEN

There I was on the sister island with no job and no money. One day, I saw a job ad in the newspaper: Typist wanted for a small business. I applied, but there was one not-so-minor issue. I couldn't type. Not one bit. *And here I was calling the number and arranging an interview for the typist job!*

When I got there for my interview, the second or third question was obvious.

"How quickly do you type?"

"I don't," I answered.

Here's the twist: I convinced the lady in charge to hire me and teach me how to type. She knew I really wanted the job—*and needed a break*—and I explained that I was new in the country, behind in my rent, and desperately needed the money. I asked her to give me one chance, and I don't even remember exactly what she said, but I can still see the look in her eyes. She made me feel seen. She saw something in me, and it wasn't just desperation. It was willpower combined with the kind of work ethic that would come in handy. Somewhere along the line, she found her answer: yes.

I'm telling you this story for one simple reason: If I had never applied for that job, my trajectory would be far different. I was honest about what I couldn't do, which is also quite the badass move in life. I could have lied and typed with one finger for a few days before getting fired, but I didn't go that route. The lying would have been my downfall. The truth got me that job. My work ethic kept it.

I remember my mother saying to someone once, "If something happens, Judy will always tell you the truth." Honesty is one of my core values. It goes along with taking responsibility for your actions—

and your first action is always the truth. I learned early on that I will always tell the truth, no matter what the consequences are in life. The only time I might lie is if my life were at stake. What else can you do to me if I tell the truth?

My clients, friends, and loved ones know they will get the truth from me. It's a great place to start and maintain all your relationships.

In the case of my first real job, my boss actually taught me how to type. Somewhere, somehow, she felt that I was honest, teachable, smart, eager to do a good job, and that I truly needed that employment. My gratitude would make me excel each day.

It was all potential—and that's what she hired.

It was a good starting point, although life would test me along the way.

A CONVERSATION WITH YOURSELF

When you are starting anything new, stop telling yourself:

- Life's not fair.

- Others have more than me.

- I don't have what it takes.

Instead, start telling yourself:

- I can do this.

- This is what I was created for.

- I am unfiltered and unapologetic in the pursuit of my dreams.

NOTES
FOR YOUR JOURNEY

CHAPTER THREE

The Badass Tests Herself

Picture it: A young woman is in a new place, navigating the job market for the first time. She is thrilled with her early typing job, but it doesn't pay enough to live on, so she must move on. That was me. At my next job, I found myself with a boss who was crass, rude, and condescending to the workers. To put it simply, I just didn't like the way he would speak to people.

I was still that same social justice type who fought for her friends, and even strangers, when there was any inkling of injustice, but there wasn't much I could do to change the tone of that workplace except quit. And so that's exactly what I did, which wasn't the most financially prudent decision. Being young, my options were limited, but I found a new job with a business that promised assistance when it came to getting a US visa.

Not only am I justice minded, but I'm also an inquisitive person. I knew something didn't feel right. When I peeled back very few layers, I realized that the actual business at hand involved collecting money and promising US visas … only the visas never really happened. My new boss spent all the money he collected while delivering nothing in return.

I started to make behind-the-scenes calls to the customers, asking them about receivables. There wasn't one person who actually got a visa. When the boss wasn't looking, I'd call people and say in a low voice, "Listen, I work for XYZ Company. Please don't make any more payments. You should even try to get your money back and report this to the authorities."

There was no choice but to leave another job, which isn't easy when you need that paycheck desperately. The good news is that I wasn't a part of this scam. I just worked in the business's office, but I couldn't allow it to go on any longer, with my daily work hours contributing to this disaster.

UNAPOLOGETIC:

There is no amount of money that's worth compromising your values. If it feels wrong, it is wrong, and your move is to remove yourself from the situation. Immediately. If it feels like a no, it is a no. Don't force it to be a yes.

The fallout for me was serious. Jobs weren't easy to find in those days, and I didn't have any education past high school. What happened was the worst possible scenario: I didn't work for a long time.

My days were spent scouring the help wanted section of the newspaper, followed by endless cold calls where I'd hear, "No, we aren't hiring."

No one was hiring. This wasn't good news to a young woman with no real net to catch her if she fell. At the time, Miss Natalie and I began sharing a home with another young woman. The monthly rent became a constant worry, along with basic needs such as food money. My roommates were beyond understanding, but I knew their kindness could only last so long. They were young and struggling too, and they couldn't carry another person, despite my best efforts to find a job.

My next unfiltered move: I stopped myself from going down a negativity spiral. During the bleak moments, I reached inward and realized I wasn't alone.

I grew up in church, and prayer has always been an important and amazing part of my life. Even as a young adult, I would read Psalms and pray every night, knowing that *things will get better because they always have, always will.*

One Friday night, I was praying and said, "God, this upcoming week has to be better. I can't do this anymore. I *have* to get a job. Please help me."

I was very specific as the prayer continued. "God," I said, "by nine o'clock Monday morning, something has to happen for me with a new job."

There were no cell phones in those days, so early Monday morning, my ear was glued to the landline phone in our living room.

9:00 a.m.

The phone rang as I glanced at the time.

"God, I really need this today," I rushed before I lifted the phone receiver. "Hello."

Just one hello can change your entire life.

"Good morning, could I please speak with Judy Mahalia Jack?" asked this lovely lady on the other end of the line.

"This is Judy."

"I received your resume, and I'm wondering if you can come in tomorrow for a job interview?"

If I could come in tomorrow? I could come in right now! Just the word *job* followed by the word *interview* had my heart doing a dance.

I wrote down the directions and went to prepare for the interview the next day.

Let me back this up a bit. I'd had the good luck of meeting Hasely Crawford—Trinidad's first Olympic gold medalist and a champion of the 100- and 200-meter dash, who won a bronze medal in the 1976 summer games for the 100-meter track and field race—and who also happened to be friends with Miss Natalie.

One evening, Hasely and I were chatting about our lives and the striking similarities in our pasts. He was one of eleven children and had gone through many hardships, including pulling his hamstring and then making a major comeback due to sheer will. A kind, sensitive man, he seemed genuinely interested in hearing my story. Many times in life, we clam up and don't allow people to get to know us. But I wanted to tell my story and listen to other people's sagas. So, I told him about growing up as number eight out of ten in a large family, moving to a new country, and my recent struggles to secure employment. I even told him about the job I was forced to quit because it just wasn't right to stay there.

"Give me your resume, Judy. Let me give it to this lady I met when I was at training the other day," he offered. "Maybe she has an opportunity."

There are two ways to go when someone offers help. You can think, *Yeah, sure, whatever,* while convincing yourself that nothing good will come out of this because of past disappointments.

Or you can hustle and give that fantastic athlete your resume!

UNAPOLOGETIC:

There is no shame in asking for help. When someone offers, take it. When you can give help, offer it. Believe in people's higher selves while projecting positivity onto their intentions.

It was Hasely's contact calling me that Monday morning. As I was prepping for the interview, a funny thing happened: I realized I had no proper shoes! My everyday shoes weren't appropriate at all, so I had to borrow shoes from one of my roommates (there are many pluses in living with a group of young women, and shoes are one of them).

Shoe emergency resolved, I did the interview and got the job! I started right away. It was a temporary position for the receptionist who had gone on maternity leave, and I was hired to stand in for her while she was gone. It was a steady paycheck for a short period. Instead of coasting, I cleared up all her backlog of work, to the delight of my superiors. What threw it over the edge was that I'm a fast learner and can usually figure out the solutions as I go along. I can tinker and figure out how things work. I would stay late and eat lunch at my desk for a reason. When the receptionist returned from her maternity leave, I was told that because of my work ethic, they were keeping me permanently. It wasn't long before I was transferred to their warehouse as a full-time clerk, which was actually a promotion over the receptionist job.

On my own time, I learned the company's software inside and out. In addition, I became friends with the consultant, named Sallian, who was hired to maintain the software. When she came to the warehouse to check if everything was working, I'd ask her questions, and she would take me through the latest in tech updates. We grew to be friends, too. Sallian guided me, mentored me, advised me, and at times, even mothered me, which felt nice because I was all alone in a new country. I am who I am today in business and in life because of her wonderful drive, caring nature, and relentless pursuit of doing her best work.

It wasn't long before another company was looking to put someone on staff who would be responsible for that particular software. Thanks to my clerk work and what I had learned from Sallian, I got that job and worked with the company for a period until, one day, I got an opportunity that was an easy yes. Sallian had decided to go out on her own as a consultant after she had received the rights to that software and various other programs.

"I want you to work for me," she said.

The new company had a staff of two: Sallian and me. She knew I could (and would) do the work of four people tirelessly and without complaining. It was imperative to hit the ground running and learn quickly because she already had plenty of clients. I was up for the challenge.

A BADASS BETTERS HERSELF

I always had the desire to better myself by earning a university degree. After high school graduation, I wasn't able to continue my education because there was no money to send me to school. The story could have ended there, as it did for a lot of people. After high school, most of us start working and push aside the need for additional education because of the financial issues, plus the lack of time. Obtaining a college degree went deeper for me. The truth was that I always felt like I didn't have what it takes to go to university, and perhaps it was for the best that my scholarly life didn't include university courses.

This type of thinking changed while I was working with Sallian and our clients. I was seeing the opportunities higher education could afford, and I could hear my mother in my mind: "It's really your ticket to freedom."

One day, I saw my ticket in the form of an ad for a summer program at the prestigious University of the West Indies, where you could earn your bachelor's degree in a three-year time period. I applied for a spot but figured that this dream seemed like an impossibility.

Why am I even doing this? I asked myself as I wrote the check for $50 to be "considered." And truly, what were they even considering?

I don't have anything they're asking for in this laundry list of demands for potential students, I lamented to myself.

I didn't have the background, the previous high school core classes, or a certain score on necessary exams. I had never even taken those tests. You were required to have already taken particular courses if you chose to go into their business or science programs. The lowest number of those subjects I needed to get into the university was five. I had four and a half. So close, but not enough.

Something inside of me filled out the forms and wrote the check. I knew the odds were against me, but that was the story of my young life. There would be no excuses to not try. Sure, it had a good chance of not working, but still there was always that lingering hope.

I applied for the University of West Indies in the same way I interviewed for that typing job when I didn't type. There is that "can do" spark in my soul that refuses to count myself out.

That's why they're called odds. Life can be a game of chance.

Time passed, the check was cashed, and I heard nothing from the university. Even though I knew there was nothing I could do to speed up their decision, I got to the point where I couldn't stand it any longer. I called the admissions office to check on my status.

"Name?" asked the woman on the other end of the line.

I gave her my information, and she pulled up my admissions form. And then she asked me a question that seemed odd because she already had the answer in her hands.

"Do you think you got in?" she inquired.

Wait, I'm the one who was supposed to ask the questions.

"No," I said quickly. "I don't think so."

"Of course, you got through. Welcome to university," she said.

UNAPOLOGETIC:

Get rid of your "I can't" mentality. Think: "Why not me?" Commit to trying despite the odds against you. Then keep trying. That's all life is. The worst that can happen is you get rejected. If it's a no, then it's a no. If it's a yes, it's a wonderful turn of events. By the way, I've hardly ever applied for a job where I didn't get it— qualified or not.

The girl with no food as a child had become a university student! At the time, I was making enough money working with Sallian to move into my own two-bedroom apartment and go to university. Even the idea of a higher education filled me with visions of what could be possible for my life moving forward.

There was only one problem—I didn't have the entire desired academic background. But the school saw something in me that was worthwhile. Attitude is everything. If you think you can … you can.

My time at the University of West Indies was wonderful and showed me the importance of teamwork and opening myself up to creative solutions.

Obstacles were everywhere, but there was always a different way to approach a problem. Something's not working? Try another way.

For example, one of my tougher subjects was math. I see a math class and working with numbers in the world as totally different things. I see math class as perplexing algebra, geometry, and trig, but I'm not afraid of numbers in the world. In fact, I excel at accounting and planning a budget. I had a hard time with math coursework in high school, and now this business major was confronted by university math, which was like a foreign language to me. One Sunday, I was frantic about my first official major math exam, which was scheduled the next day. I was at home, trying my best to learn the formulas, ready to hit my head against the wall when one of my classmates called me.

"Let me test you, Judy," he said. "I want to make sure you know those formulas."

Teamwork. They don't have a formal course on it, but the biggest lesson I learned at university was how life is sweeter when we help each other.

I had several amazing classmates whom I remain grateful for even now. We would trade our skills and tutor each other in our tough subjects. I may have needed help in math, but I was always a voracious reader and good at English courses. One of my friends was a geologist, and I helped him with his written papers while he explained tougher science concepts. We worked through it all together, which was the best way of making good use of all the resources.

And we still had fun at university, although we were young adults in our mid-twenties. We weren't that young in comparison with the other students, but we weren't that old, either. I found that university life came naturally for me, and I learned the lessons of a lifetime.

Namely, that filling out that seemingly random form could be my best badass move.

A CONVERSATION WITH YOURSELF

How to make it *not* work:

- Wait for opportunities to come to you in your living room. Between commercials.

- Don't network. Forget meeting new people.

- Stay within your comfort zone.

- Ignore red flags.

- Don't trust your intuition.

- Fear the idea of trying.

How to make it *work*:

- Put yourself out there. A five-minute chat could change your life.

- Apply for jobs beyond your skill level. You can learn on the job.

- Trust your intuition about workplace ethics.

- Reach out for help, bartering with your own skills. A quid pro quo is always badass.

- Embrace the challenge of trying.

NOTES
FOR YOUR JOURNEY

CHAPTER FOUR

You Gotta Love the Unfiltered You

A little bit later in my life, I would meet Chaplain Goldson, who is a wonderful older man from Jamaica. Each time I would see him, my self-esteem would get a booster shot that I wish I could bottle for everyone.

"You are a thoroughbred," he told me.

The next time, he smiled and insisted, "You come from a long lineage of good stock."

At yet another unforeseen meeting, he told me, "You are an eagle. You are not meant to run around with the chickens."

Short and sweet self-esteem booster shots. What's not to love?

Chaplain Goldson saw something in me long before I could have ever seen it in myself, and I made the choice each time to believe in his version. This meant pushing past my own self-doubts and normal feelings of being inadequate or "imposter syndrome." He amplified the good, expanded the positive, and strengthened my core belief that I was indeed special, worthy, and even magical. He crowned me a badass (without ever saying those words, because he was a religious man), and he believed in my strength, determination, and God-given skills. Many of us spend a lifetime downplaying those things instead of pumping ourselves up emotionally.

I want to say these words to you now as I pay it forward: You are an eagle. You were made in the image of your Creator, and She is absolutely gorgeous and giving.

Do you believe me? It's OK if my words gave you a bit of a pause.

As young girls, we're often taught to take a backseat and hide our talents, smarts, and achievements. Blowing your own horn is known in some circles as bragging or self-involvement, which is then dubbed an extremely unattractive trait. The badass in me calls BS. Don't dare cower and make yourself small while denying your talents and natural abilities.

Get that positive internal dialogue going. Go to the mirror, look at that gorgeous woman or girl staring back at you, and tell yourself that you are worth taking a chance on. You can do this. You are smart and capable. You have the answers. You will trust yourself. All it takes is that first step.

"You have greatness within you," says Les Brown.

Let me ask you: What greatness can you see within yourself at this moment in time? It's the first step when it comes to loving yourself unapologetically. You must pinpoint what you love and then work to make it even greater.

PUTTING YOU FIRST

During the safety briefings on an airplane, they tell you that in the case of an extreme drop in cabin pressure, you must place the oxygen mask on yourself first, before assisting others. There is a reason for this order. If you don't put your mask on first, there is a good chance that you will pass out from lack of oxygen before you are able to help anyone, including yourself. It is the same way with life. If you don't get *your* shit together, how are you going to help anyone else? If you are no good to you, you are incapable of being much good to anyone else.

Your self-worth permeates every encounter you have in both your work and your personal life, especially in how you express love to others. See if this mantra sounds familiar: "I love him so much. I can't imagine life without him. If he leaves me, I'll die." We'll talk about relationships more in a later chapter, but what about your own sense of self-love and self-worth? I'm not saying that a breakup can't hurt you to the core or leave you feeling depleted. I've been there. But if it leaves you with no desire or will to live anymore, then it's better it ended because the only person you should be working on a relationship with is yourself.

So, put your emotional seatbelt on first, which is a basic badass move. Learn to love yourself first before thinking about dishing it out to others. Until and unless you can confess your undying love for that awesome, badass woman in the mirror, you are incapable of loving anyone else in a profound way. This does not include the unconditional (*agape*) or enduring (*pragma*) love we have for our kids. Self-love is dependent on nothing. It just *is*. What I don't understand is, if we are capable of such deep love for our children, why can't we seem to harness just a fraction of that same love for ourselves?

What about having the same passion for our own lives? When I'm really into something, I tend to become a bit obsessed with it. It doesn't matter what it is; if it's my current fixation, I will go all in, and I will give it my all. I remember even when I partied as a young woman, I did so with wild abandon. I'm not the type to leave anything on the table, because this is my one and only life story.

UNAPOLOGETIC:

My motto has been the same since I was fifteen years old: "Go big or stay home." It worked for me then, and it still holds true today.

Naturally, there were times when I didn't feel like I had any unfiltered DNA in my system. There were times when I wondered if anything made sense and asked myself, "What is the value in living?" I had lost touch with my soul and my Source. Most of all, I had lost touch with myself, and I needed to find my way back home, but not to a physical address—to the home I carry in my heart.

One day, I wandered into a church and, sitting before the Eucharist, I began to pray and … cry. At that point in my life, I was feeling really, really lost and disconnected. I felt so alone. The more I prayed, the more I cried. To this day, I don't know why I cried, but maybe it was a form of cleansing. I do know that, after that experience, I felt light as a feather and free as a bird. It brought me back to where I needed to be. It was the beginning of the conversation I needed to start having with myself about a concept known as self-love.

Today, there is no one on this earth who can tell me anything disparaging about myself and cause me to internalize whatever darkness they are handing off. I may pause to see if it makes sense and to evaluate if there is a part of me that requires growth. If I find it useful, I use it, and if I don't, I just discard it and move on. I tell myself every day that I am enough. I am enough for me. I may not be enough for anyone else, but that is not my concern. I am enough for me, so I can be enough for my girls, my family, and my friends—and also for my clients, whom I lead by example. After many different career turns,

I eventually opened my own consulting business, and as a business owner, it was more important than ever to be able to lean boldly into my own self-worth as I helped my clients.

UNFILTERED:

Being good to yourself starts with accepting yourself and all your God-given attributes. So what if your nose is flat and broad, if your butt is big (people pay good money these days to get one of those, actually!) or if it's flat? If you are a darker shade than your sisters or the shortest one in the room—so what? You are uniquely you. Perfect in every way, every day.

What makes you who you are is a lot more than just your physical attributes. It's your character, your morals, your belief system, and your thoughts. Who you are on the inside is what matters most. The outside makes you recognizable, but the inside makes you memorable.

I am sure you know of someone who is, by society's definition, beautiful, but they are "character dirty." By this, I mean people who are nice and pretty on the outside but are mean and ugly on the inside. They are unkind and move through this world without thinking about others. We look at these seemingly beautiful people and wish we could be like them, but we don't know their story, do we? Would we really like to be like them if we knew how they felt deep down?

I want you to embrace all of you—look in the mirror and remind yourself every single day of just how freaking fabulous you are, were, and will be in the future.

UNAPOLOGETIC:

How you see yourself, the image you have of you, is a huge determining factor in where you go in life—or where you don't go or never will, for that matter.

AN EXERCISE

I want you to take a piece of paper or find a journal that can accompany this book. Flip to a fresh page and draw a line down the middle. On one side, write: "What Makes Me Unique." On the other side, write: "Qualities I Wish to Develop." Then, I want you to spend some quiet time thinking about your qualities that should be listed in each column. When you are finished, take time to read it and allow yourself to soak it all in. Don't be shy. Anything that you really enjoy about yourself—what makes you proud of you—write it down. It's an ongoing list. You can just keep adding to it.

Finally, go to the mirror; take a good look at yourself and read your unique qualities aloud, then read the qualities you wish to develop. What do you need to do differently to develop those qualities? Jot down a few of those ideas and read them several times a week in front of that mirror, or just to yourself.

It's about time you embrace your power so you can live and lead your best life. You must take action to change your life. Just thinking about it won't be enough. You must do something about it by making an action plan.

Write down one new step each day that will get you closer to your life goals. Look at this list on a regular basis and write down practical ways to approach these steps.

AN IMAGE HOLLYWOOD CREATED

A lot of our negative self-image comes from false conditioning or what we see on TV or in the movies. Hollywood has defined for us what beauty should look like, how it should walk, and how it should talk. I want you to know that Hollywood is made up of Photoshop, talented makeup artists, and designers who know the best ways to hide flaws. It's not real, yet many of us hate ourselves for not living up to some impossible standard.

The truth is that we all have unique physical qualities—great hair, beautiful eyes, large pores, acne, stretch marks, cellulite, a great booty, killer arms, big hips, beautiful lips, fine lines showing a life well lived—the list goes on and on. What I've learned is that beauty isn't skin deep. For me, beauty isn't what we see on the outside but what comes from our inner core and who we are. It's about who we are and not what we look like. Why not just be happy with who you are and let that be a reason to celebrate?

There are other easy but profound ways to improve your self-esteem.

One thing that has helped me on my self-improvement journey is deepening my spirituality through meditation. I fell in love with it, and it has become the medicine for all of my psychological ailments. My thoughts create my life, so my thinking must be harmonious. Another thing that helps me with my self-esteem is practicing gratitude. When I'm having a particularly challenging day, I intentionally look for things to be grateful for, and by the time I'm done being grateful, I feel so much better. Similarly, one more habit I've developed to boost my own self-esteem is blessing others. As I'm driving or walking, I send a silent blessing to all I meet.

You might think that's too many people, but remember, the more you give, the more you're likely to receive. I am a firm believer in universal consciousness. I know the vibes I send out to the Universe come back to me because I can feel it in the way all these habits boost my self-esteem.

I challenge you to love yourself. Get that internal love dialogue going before you do.

NEGATIVE SELF-TALK

One day, as if she were some supreme deity, my high school principal said to me, "Judy Jack, your days are numbered."

Hello! Can you please repeat that one? Or maybe you should never say it again …

My mind raced. What was that supposed to mean? *My days are numbered … in what way? Am I being kicked out of school? Am I going to leave this world? Is someone going to physically hurt me? And why is my principal involved?* The truth is that adults often say things without pondering the unnecessary pain and fear they inflict upon little innocent minds and hearts. Words count, and harsh, untethered words wound.

She said this to me after I'd mouthed off to my teacher. We were lining up for assembly, and young Judy wasn't in that line because I was always talking to people. Always talking! That was my offense, and there was only a judge and no jury.

"Your days are numbered." And she used my first and last name, which made it even more serious!

Emotionally, I suffered in silence, as so many children do on a daily basis. It wasn't long before my every thought, action, and deed demonstrated that I truly did believe my days were numbered. That upcoming test? What did it matter? My days were numbered. Holiday break? Would I make it to that date? Now, I jokingly look back at that time in my life and think, *It was only my mother's prayers that added more numbers to my days!*

I get it now. My principal wanted to give me a stern warning that my days of not following the rules were numbered. Perhaps she chose her words poorly when she threatened my life with this language, if you look at it from the brain of a teenager. But it's those little moments, and others, that stick—that make us feel that we are unlovable, unworthy, and unwanted.

We must remember that words are powerful. They cut like a sword and do something much more inconspicuous, too: erode our self-esteem. My view of self was strong, even for a teenager, so I would recover. But what about another child who was on far shakier ground? What about the twenty- or thirty-year-old woman whose partner tells her, "You're nothing"? Or when her mother says, "You're such a disappointment to me"? We should be mindful before we say something to someone of any age. The flip side is that we need to develop a love of ourselves so as not to internalize bombshell comments that work against our higher good.

Though they do not leave physical cuts and scars, these words plant and embed themselves deep in our subconscious and set the standard for what other words and thoughts will flourish there. If fed in a positive way, a garden might spring forth and leave a way for wonderful things to grow, prosper, and rise out of us. However, if fed negativity and doubt, weeds will quickly spread and likely consume much of the good that attempts to flower in their midst.

We must be careful of the words we speak, as well as take care of how we receive the words spoken over us. We need to discern when to allow them to take root and eventually flower, and when they should be discarded to keep from spoiling the rest of the fruit.

"Your days are numbered" set my life on its trajectory as the phrase rooted itself and allowed weeds into my garden. This meant there would be more work to be done to till the soil later on in order to create an environment where good things would grow and thrive again.

Even my physical being suffered immensely during this time of self-doubt and fear. Even despite the occasional food insecurity, my eating habits began to vary widely, and I clearly remember one point where I was hardly eating anything at all. Eventually, my eating habits shifted again. I ate and drank everything, and my weight suddenly ballooned out of my control. In my attempt to get a handle on it, I started yo-yo dieting. There is no diet or exercise fad known to man that I didn't try. As with all fad diets, I would lose the weight for a little while, and then it would come back with a vengeance. This, and a slew of other destructive behaviors, went on for years until, one day, I finally decided enough was enough.

Remember my conversation with myself that started on that day when I was crying my heart out in the church? Well, that was just the start. I needed many more hard conversations with myself to get real if I was going to make it out alive. I was sick and tired of being a fool, doubting myself, and allowing my fears to paralyze me. At age twenty-seven, I was suddenly done with telling myself that I was not good enough. I just got fed up with not living my best life. I knew there was more out there, but how could I find it?

LEARNING TO LOVE YOURSELF

If you do the same thing again and again and it's not working, the most life-changing commitment you can make is to do something differently. My starting point for doing things differently was my internal dialogue, which I knew had to change from a place of self-doubt to self-empowerment. *My days are not numbered; they are just beginning. I will stand up for friends in need, even if it costs me. I will follow the rules, but I will make my own rules as well. My days are not numbered; my doubts are numbered now.*

I had to reverse the things I believed about myself to adjust my thinking so that my internal conversations could be different. If we want different in our lives, then we must think differently, act differently, and be different. Everything in life starts with a single thought. It follows that you can change your life in the very next minute with your next thought. Reframe your thinking and you will change your life.

FROM SELF-LOVE TO REAL LOVE

Until you truly see and accept yourself, you'll keep looking for validation in all the wrong places. I spent years doing that dance—thinking if I could just be prettier, thinner, smarter, or more successful, then I'd finally be worthy of love.

Remember that principal who told me my days were numbered? Those words stuck with me far longer than they should have. But here's the thing: I had to learn to write my own story. The same way I stood up to that principal back then, I had to stand up to the voice in my head that said I wasn't enough.

That fire release ceremony I mentioned earlier? It wasn't just about letting go of old hurts. It was about making space for something better—real love, starting with loving myself. When I burned those letters, I wasn't just releasing pain. I was declaring that I deserved more than relationships built on shaky ground.

Look at yourself in the mirror. Really look. That woman staring back at you has everything she needs to build the life she wants. She doesn't need anyone else's approval or permission to shine. When you finally get that—*really* get it—you'll stop accepting less than you deserve in relationships.

A CONVERSATION WITH YOURSELF

Stop telling yourself:

- I am unlovable.

- I am damaged goods.

- I am not enough.

Start telling yourself:

- I am freaking fabulous and gorgeous!

- I am hella sexy and smart!

- I am totally unfiltered and unapologetic!

NOTES
FOR YOUR JOURNEY

CHAPTER FIVE

Unfiltered in Love

Part I

In my twenties, drinking and partying were the order of my days. Living in Trinidad made that easy. I had a good job and no kids, so what else was there to do but have a good time and celebrate my freedom? I could easily party from Sunday to Sunday—and this included drinking, smoking, and dancing with interesting young men. Life was fantastic, and I was living in the fast lane. Literally.

I remember leaving a party at five o'clock one morning to take someone to the airport. I was tired and halfway drunk and wanted to see if I could make the speedometer in my car reach dizzying speeds. I remember laughing to myself and thinking, *Gosh, I feel so free doing this!* You know that God is good, right? She protects children, drunks, and fools. I was two out of those three that morning. I was also lucky to survive.

Love would prove to be the next dizzying ride.

MY FIRST MARRIAGE

I met Brian when I was twenty. My roommate had a boyfriend who was in the Coast Guard, and Brian was his handsome friend. One day, they both showed up at our apartment, and it was one of those magical evenings where you sit, drink wine, talk, and laugh. Brian and I exchanged numbers, one thing led to another, and we started going out. We eventually fell in love and moved in together.

"You're living together … what's next?"

"Do we hear wedding bells?"

Friends would ask us that all the time, but I was never someone who felt I had to be on a certain life schedule crafted by others.

However, the nudges worked. We decided to get married because that seemed like the next right thing. But deep down, I had my doubts about marriage. One day, I remember saying to Brian, "I don't think I can do this. I don't think I'm ready for marriage." Turns out, Brian was more securely on the expectation treadmill than I was in those days. He talked me out of my doubts and convinced me that our marriage would be "the next great thing" for both of us.

"You're just nervous," he said. Correct! I was petrified.

There were days when I thought, *I have to get out of this. What the hell am I doing?* My inner voice would scream, *Who will you get to marry you? Are you even worthy enough?* We doubt ourselves so much. We think we're lucky if someone takes an interest in us. So, yes, I figured maybe I should just go ahead and marry him, not giving any thought to what I really wanted.

I was at a stage of my life where I believed in myself to a point, but when it came to love and relationships, I always felt unloved. I really felt as if I should marry Brian because maybe no one else would come along. So, I went against everything I felt and decided to get married. Don't get me wrong—I loved Brian very much, and we had plenty of fun together. But was that enough to marry him, or anyone else for that matter?

I should have honored my instincts. I believe there is a higher Source, a higher consciousness, that governs our lives. It offers us all the pauses we need to avoid making foolish or really bad decisions. Think of it as a warning light in a car. You see the light blinking amber, and if you don't pay attention, then it's not long before you're broken down on the side of the road.

My entire life was headed for the ditch.

HERE COMES THE BRIDE ... THERE GOES THE PRIEST

On my wedding day, I was late. Let's take a moment here. I was no later than any other bride might be. So what? *A lot*, it turned out.

My younger brother was supposed to drive me to the church, but he had some delays picking me up. I swear I was ready and waiting.

When I finally arrived at the church, everyone was standing outside, looking sad.

The priest had left the building!

"He ... left?" I asked. I was stunned.

The priest had other commitments and was gone!

My initial thought: *Great, I've been saved!*

"OK," is what I said instead. I was a badass problem solver, even when thrown a serious life curve. "Why don't we just go to the reception, have fun, and not get married?" I suggested. "Maybe this is not supposed to happen. Perhaps this is God's way of saying no, or not yet. But we can certainly enjoy the party!"

There are signs in life. Clear signs. The priest leaving sounds like a movie plot and not real life. One must pay attention, because this started with my hesitation and then my lateness to the biggest day of my life. My body was saying "don't" when the people in my life were begging me to say "I do."

In the end, there is something about being a woman standing in a white dress in front of a church that prevents people from clearly seeing the signs. They thought I was sad, but honestly, I was dancing on the inside. They all thought we should still get married no matter what. They saw this as a minor inconvenience. One of my friends went into action, calling around until she found a priest who could perform the ceremony. *Sigh.* I am still wondering why I wasn't strong enough to just say no and leave it at that.

The other priest eventually arrived, and Brian and I were married. Even after the ceremony, when we were all laughing and having fun at the reception, amid the congratulations and best wishes, I couldn't help thinking, *This shit is funny! Like, really, your priest walked out on you! How messed up do you have to be for that to happen?*

This was my reality on what was supposed to be the happiest day of my life. In retrospect, I'm sure now that it was a message from the Universe, but at the time, I was thinking, *I'm just unlucky that I got to the church late. My nerves are causing the doubts. Yes, this day was really messed up, but we fixed it.*

Or did we?

On the plus side, Brian was an amazing guy, and I loved him. He was smart and funny, two things that I was looking for in a romantic partner. He had this way of winning me over—at least in the moment—every single time we had a disagreement or were at a crossroads.

But we had one major issue that I just couldn't get past. I am your classic overachiever, and I am always looking for ways to be better. The issue was that Brian was quite happy staying right where we were. I now know for sure that love alone is not enough to sustain a marriage. Partners must have at least one common goal they are working toward. You must have certain conversations with your partner before you commit, as those "before" conversations can save you a lifetime of heartache and headaches. Have the talk about money, kids, family values, and goals, as these are the issues that will loom larger than life in your relationship.

As I wrote at the beginning of this chapter, I like to have a good time. And once Brian and I got married, we continued to party, but as I matured in age and life experience, I wanted so much more out of my life than good times and drinking. I wanted to get my degree, to have a family, to travel and see the world. I wanted to make a name for myself through my work and create a meaningful legacy. My husband just wanted another party, and one was always available to him, seven nights a week. We saw life through different lenses, and that was the beginning of the end.

Society teaches us to stay the course in marriage, no matter what, but I was betraying myself, losing my soul and worrying that my ambition would go next—making excuses and compromising my ambitions— including my dream of earning my university education. College, and all the time it would take for me to study, wasn't what Brian had in mind for us. That was work. It didn't mesh with staying out until dawn.

I had to choose: stay in a failing marriage or leave before losing myself completely. I chose to leave, although Brian ultimately made the decision easy. Around the same time, I found out that he had been cheating on me and the other woman was pregnant with his child. My God, it hurts to the core—*even now.* Some deceptions leave a permanent mark, and this would sketch a deep scar that had everything to do with the betrayal of your best friend and life partner.

At one point, when his cheating had been confirmed and before I knew about the pregnancy, I even offered to "make a baby."

"You're not ready for a child," Brian told me.

Talk about that Sexy Diva of the Universe looking out for me!

YOU CAN'T KEEP HIM, AND WHY TRY?

It astounds me that, as women, we often act so foolishly to try to keep a man. You cannot *keep* a man. He stays if he wants to stay, and that's all there is to it. Nothing you try or concoct or promise will ever make him stay if he doesn't want to be there. He can be physically present while, at the same time, emotionally absent. One of the most heartbreaking pains in the world is sharing a bed with someone who has become a stranger.

Unfortunately, my story is not unique. It's all too common for strong, accomplished, badass ladies to say that their romantic relationships are not fulfilling or are even mentally exhausting. We keep telling ourselves that it's us, that we need to be fixed. "If only I lose some weight ... If only I pay more attention to his needs ... If only I spend more time ... get Botox, buy that dress, try that trick in bed ... then he'll notice me. He'll love me. He'll stop cheating."

UNFILTERED:

Hell NO! You are not the cause of his behavior. You are his spouse, not his damn mother. Do not degrade yourself or make yourself feel like you need to do more for a man who is undeserving. If he does not appreciate you the way you are and support where you might want to go, he is not worth your time, energy, or emotions.

CALLING IT QUITS

I got so fed up with my husband's behavior that I initiated the divorce, paid for it, and went with him to collect the divorce papers. I wanted out so badly that I was determined for him to get those papers and sign them as quickly as possible. I was, quite literally, sick and tired of being sick and tired. I decided the only way I could start living the life that I deserved would be to clean up my act and make some major changes. If I wanted something different, then I had to do things differently.

In all honesty, if he hadn't cheated, I don't know if I would have left him. Maybe it was supposed to happen this way. I don't think the bad parts were predestined, but some people come into your life for a season. The issue arises when we take that season and try to make it into a lifetime.

I am proud that we were eventually able to handle our split with some level of maturity, recalling the friendship and love that was there at the beginning. When I initially asked him to move out, it felt as if I'd started a war with an enemy. I asked the lawyer not to serve him through a process server banging on our door but to give him the dignity of allowing him to pick up his paperwork at the lawyer's office. It felt like less of an attack. When he needed to get the papers, Brian called me and said, "Judy, can you come with me to pick up our divorce papers? I don't want to go alone."

Of course I said yes. We were best friends at one point in our lives, and I chose to focus on the good feelings that lingered.

I remember when we went to collect the papers from the registry, the guy who was serving us asked who was getting divorced, and we said, "Us."

"Are you sure about this?" he asked us.

We walked in laughing and talking and walked out the same way. We never had any real animosity after we separated—even with his cheating. None. It remains one of the aspects of my life for which I am most grateful. I rose above my anger.

After my divorce, I was thirty and convinced I would roam through the rest of my life alone. I was in this emotional void and was sure that I would never find anyone. This isn't badass thinking, but grief talking. There are times in life when you just have to deal with the sadness of what was, move forward, and try to get your head above water again.

The truth is that all I wanted to do at this point was have fun, but deep down, I was sad. My star sign is Aries, and one of Aries' toxic traits is sticking things out to the end, even to our detriment, because we are "fixers." Feelings of personal unworthiness and failure dominated me for some time ... and then I met John, who is my current husband. I wasn't looking for a relationship; I just wanted to have fun. I had already made up my mind that I would never marry again.

We often jump into new relationships before healing from trauma. I wish I'd known then what I know now. I wish I'd given myself those years after my divorce to heal the parts of me that I didn't want to face.

UNFILTERED:

Ladies, my advice to you: Take the time to know who you are and take the time to heal. Life is not running away, nor is your clock ticking. You are worth every damn minute of that time.

With John, our relationship was a little more serious because he was older. He asked me many times to marry him, and I always said no. I would jokingly say to him that I am not marriage material. Just as I was feeling good about myself and my decision not to ever get married again, one conversation with a friend brought up all those feelings of unworthiness again. We were over at her house, having dinner, and she asked me if I was going to get married to John, to which I told her what I'd been telling him: no.

"Judy, do you see how John looks at you?" she asked me. "I don't think you will ever find anyone again who will look at you this way."

In the back of my mind, I thought, *Maybe she's right.*

John and I got married on September 14, 2002, in a beautiful ceremony in a church with very close friends and family. It was a small wedding filled with love. I was thirty-three years old and ready to settle down.

Or was I?

The thought that kept running through my mind was that I didn't want to get to eighty years old and be alone. Because I came from a single-parent home, I did not want a repeat of that. Our minds play these crazy tricks on us based on the way we were conditioned. We must question these thoughts to see if they are valid. I would go so far as to wager that none of those thoughts are valid or helpful.

A CONVERSATION WITH YOURSELF

Stop telling yourself:

- Your love life must follow others' timetables.

- Marriage is the only successful relationship outcome.

- You need a partner to be complete.

Start telling yourself:

- I choose my own self-worth, with or without a partner.

- My needs matter in all relationship decisions.

- I will honor both love and its endings.

NOTES
FOR YOUR JOURNEY

CHAPTER SIX

Unfiltered in Love

Part II

There is an identity crisis that plagues women. It's the way we lose ourselves in our romantic relationships to the point where our original self doesn't even exist anymore—either in whole or in part. I'm all for adapting and changing, but at what price?

We've all been there—when you first fall in love, and every single thing in your life seems to revolve around that other person and their dreams, wishes, and desires. You're in the haze of something new, special, and wonderful with the lingering question, "Is this The One?" Maybe you are even lost in love as thoughts of "the next step" linger in the back of your brain. Are you thinking of white dresses? Listening to love songs? Buying into the idea that "The two shall become one"?

Nothing's wrong with those thoughts, and it's not that I want to rain on anyone's love parade, but sometimes love is just not enough.

My question to you is this: What happens to *you* in this love scenario?

UNAPOLOGETIC:

Who you are—who we are as women—is so much more than the person or people in our lives, including our deepest loves. Love freely, but don't lose yourself in the process. You don't want to wake up one day and wonder, Where did I go?

Many of us define our entire identity through our romantic relationships. While finding love and support is wonderful, I've learned that losing yourself can destroy both you and the relationship.

Even after saying "I do," you're still individuals. Whether it's marriage or any serious romantic union, there's always pressure from others to reach that finish line—especially when you're dating someone your parents actually like (which, in many cases, is classified as "A Really Big Deal").

I DO. DO I?

Three months into dating, you're still in the "getting to know each other beyond the surface stuff" phase when—*oh, shit*—the world decides to weigh in.

"So, when are you going to get married? No pressure."

Heavens, just don't bring your partner to a family dinner, because then it will be like a CIA interrogation. Imagine yourself with your back against the wall in a gray room with a lone light swinging. Your parents have their questions ready: Is this serious? Did you meet your partner's parents? When will you get engaged? Are they religious? In debt? What kind of wedding do you want? Where will you live? When will you have kids? What religion? What address? What kind of life? Dogs or cats? Coke or Pepsi? It goes on and on!

"Not that we want to pry into your business, honey," says your mother when she comes up for air.

"We're just curious," says Grandma, the one who puts the "ship" in relationship.

Wait! Hold on here! I want to see my lawyer!

The only date you should be settling on after three months of dating is Italian or Mexican for dinner. No one should pressure anyone, especially not their partner, to set the date when you don't even have each other's passwords yet. Just because you look good together—him with his mortgage and great job and you with your paid-off car and rising career—that's not enough to take things to the next level. Settling down or feeling unsettled? It's your choice.

I told you about my first husband, Brian, in the last chapter, which you can now consider a cautionary tale. There was a time before we were married, when we were living together, and honestly, I thought things were fine as they were in those days. We shared a life but not a lifetime commitment. There was breathing room. It felt right in the early days ... until he introduced the concept of marriage. Looking back, I think he was being pressured by friends and family, especially those who had decided that an engagement would be the natural next step.

What utter bullshit!

In some cases, the right thing to do is to get married. However, if you marry just to make things look "right," I believe you are entering into a serious commitment for the wrong reasons and will thus build a life on a shaky foundation. This can lead to serious consequences and fractures within your relationship.

So, what do you do when well-meaning family members try to give your relationship that nudge to get it to the next level? "Things are going great as they are. Why the hell do we want to spoil it?" I have been known to say.

This is not my editorial against marriage, which is a fine institution, but simply a way to acknowledge the fact that sometimes one is not yet ready to make a major commitment. Loving someone or being exclusively committed to them is a wonderful thing. Being ready to marry that person and navigate all that comes along with those vows is another thing entirely.

You don't decide to get married by committee. Only you will know when it's right.

By the way, you can change your mind, which is common in matters of love. Sometimes, we go through our days thinking we don't want to marry or have children, and then the perfect person walks through the door, and all those decisions are back under consideration. Our lives go through natural shifts, and our needs, wants, and desires follow our evolution as humans. Only you know when your heart is going through one of these transitions. This makes it even more crucial that you are in charge of your major life choices, especially whom you marry or *if* you marry.

UNAPOLOGETIC:

No one else should set the trajectory for your future. Only you know what's right for you.

To that end, prepare to have hard conversations with close relatives and friends as you stand behind your convictions and decisions. Remember that you're not seeking permission, nor do you have to defend your decisions, especially when it comes to matters of the heart. It's your future, so *you* should always be the one steering the ship.

THE TICKING CLOCK

Many women get to a certain point in their lives when, suddenly, the big, bad biological clock starts ticking loudly. We women tend to be deadline people, and this is a big one. *The* big one. The worry is that if you miss the window, then when are those 2.5 kids, partner, and the house in the suburbs going to happen? Where is the legacy? Desperation can set in, which is not a way to live an unfiltered life. In fact, your filter should catch your worries and provide the ultimate reset.

Don't let the desire to hit a certain milestone (marriage, house, babies) force you to live and act in a manner that really doesn't suit your best interests. We believe our clock is ticking, or our gyno says something scary, and we go into a search for the almost-right or sorta-right mate to help us hit these benchmarks.

Quite often, we will be tempted to settle and choose the next person who seems reasonable in order to beat our biological clocks. So what if he has a house in foreclosure and his business life is murky? Doesn't everyone know that he's a nice guy who likes kids and dogs? You can work on the messy parts. *Right?* Wrong. Or maybe he has kids with three different women, which isn't really a dynamic you're interested in, but he's funny and handsome, and so you try to rewrite his life choices and "fix it." Danger zone! This is an easy way to wake up with a partner you wouldn't look twice at if it wasn't for your desperation.

The first person who comes along and checks a few boxes is in. "Good enough" becomes "right for me," but it never really is in the long run.

Stop the madness. This is not badass but BS. Don't live your life from a place of fear, constantly fretting that all choices are last resorts, like I once did.

Know what qualities matter most to you, prioritizing character over superficial traits. You might not find every quality, but make sure to list which are most significant. Please don't make the mistake of valuing vanity or money over honesty and integrity. And don't ever settle for less than you truly deserve because you think time is running out. Don't commit just because all of your girlfriends have entered into marrying season and you're looking around, wondering, *Where is my slice?* The winner isn't the one who showed up first but the one who will last because it works for both of you.

Life never fits into neat little compartments with set timelines, and when it doesn't, we feel like we have failed. So, we sprint headlong into the wrong relationships, willing lifetimes out of what should have only been a very short season.

Maybe *Sex and the City* put it best when Carrie said, "Some love affairs are just short stories."

IT'S YOU AND WHO?

Choose relationships carefully, building on shared values and common ground. "I have a bad picker," says Laura Dern's character in *Big Little Lies* when she finds out her husband has been cheating and has ruined their finances.

It begs the question: Who is a suitable mate? Is it Mr. Tall, Dark, and Handsome ... who is your exact opposite? You're corporate; he's a performance artist. You want to save some time for the spa and the pool on the weekends, while he wants to hike a trail and save the whales. Or is it someone just like you? You're completely compatible … yet absolutely bored because you're too similar. Can this turn into a real relationship, or is it just a fling destined to hit the skids?

We've all heard the saying that "opposites attract." That might be true in certain cases and in rom-com movies, but I'm a firm believer in being equally yoked. There is nothing worse in my book than being in a relationship with someone you have absolutely nothing in common with in life. You can barely communicate because you're so different. This will affect almost all aspects of your union, from sex to parenting to pursuing common goals.

This isn't to say that a pair of opposites can't come together in a beautiful and successful union, but it's important that you first and foremost establish common ground and a foundation to build on. Even if you have differing personalities or interests, it's still crucial to have *some* shared beliefs. These categories can fall into faith, family, or even finances. You need to have some kind of agreement in these areas, or at the very least, have an acceptable compromise or understanding up front. These are the cornerstones in most of our lives.

LOVE AND SOCIAL MEDIA

Everyone seems to have a picture-perfect life on Instagram or Facebook, including when it comes to their love relationships. Our eyes scan other people's highlight reels, which are just the sum of images they choose to show us. They're racing down the beach hand-in-hand, splashing each other in the waves, eating in the finest places with candles flickering, and jetting off to places unknown to soak up the sun and tend to their love affair.

The end result can make us feel as if we are missing out on life and love. You walk away from your phone, thinking, *What the hell is wrong with me? Why can't I find that love?*

Not a damn thing is wrong with you!

Believe me when I tell you that their grass isn't greener and their love isn't stronger. It's just filtered or edited to make you see the vibrancy that they want you to see. It's all airbrushed to give their ego a stroke and make the world believe they are experiencing relationship nirvana.

Think of it as other people putting out press releases about their so-called joy. And stop aspiring to someone else's movie version of real life.

RELATIONSHIPS 101

Life isn't like a movie where you meet cute, mate hot, marry with tears, and then walk off into the really good amber lighting of the sunset. Relationships must evolve, and no matter how long you have been together, the constant exploration of who this other person is on a soul level is time well spent. The flip side is being honest and forthcoming enough to allow them to get to know you, too. Remember that we are all constantly evolving, and the you from five years ago might be different from the you who exists now. If you love someone, the greatest gift you can give them is to take them along for the ride and love them throughout your mutual life evolutions.

As you saw in the last chapter, I've learned that happy relationships require honesty with yourself about whether a union *really* can work, and then it requires a lot of sweat equity and commitment to make it last. You can add a lot of compromise to that list, plus plenty of smiles when what you really want to do is cuss and scream. Pile on loads of laundry along with never-ending understanding, patience, and forgiveness. You must be prepared to invest all of this into your relationships if you want them to work. And even if you put in all the work and you're the most understanding person on earth with the warmest smile, and your sharing of the remote is flawless—well, love can still fail us. God knows I've had my fair share of relationship failures that hurt, but they did provide lessons in what I wanted—and what I would never do again.

UNFILTERED:

Even while investing in a relationship, you must always remember to invest in yourself. Two half people cannot make a whole relationship. This foolishness about a relationship being fifty-fifty is unhealthy. It takes two whole people to make a whole relationship and cover each other when the fifty-fifty tank is low.

COMPROMISE IS ACTUALLY BADASS (WHO KNEW?)

The relationship you build together should be anchored in the art of compromise. I say "art" here because compromise is often rooted in a vision and requires creativity. If you're just about you in life, then you should be a lone wolf. Nothing wrong with that … just don't drag someone else into it!

Being in a good relationship means it cannot be all about what you want all the time. It's the two of you, for Crimson's sake! You need to see your partner as deserving the same considerations you expect in return. You must see and acknowledge that your person deserves love, goodness, success, and a great, abundant life. Just like you do.

This is a partnership. You should be exactly that to each other—*partners*. Don't make the mistake of thinking you can make it work on your own with minimal input or feedback from your partner. That mindset is composed of a bunch of lies we have been fed. "If I work harder for it, then it will happen ..." Not exactly. You two must set common goals and each be ready to pick up the slack when needed. Sometimes the effort needed will be eighty-twenty, or sixty-forty, but you need to try to make it fifty-fifty. You must have something to work toward together. This is a necessary ingredient for success in any relationship—personal or business.

Ask yourself: What are the things you want to achieve as a couple, and do they help support your individual goals, too?

COMMUNICATION IS KEY

Anyone who has been divorced, whether once or many times (sorry), has one thing they will always list as a precursor to the breakdown of their marriage: a lack of clear communication. I can tell you from experience that nothing else in your union will work if you are not communicating effectively. The couple's mantra should be as follows: By all means, talk to me. Please do. And I will talk to you.

I've learned that communication and communion are key ingredients for any successful union—and not just basic talk, but clear, specific, precise communication. Communication must connect, build depth, and leave you both feeling understood and validated. Since neither of you can read minds, communicate clearly about your thoughts, fears, and desires.

Communication, or a lack of it, played a big role in my feelings toward relationships. Even in loving relationships, there can be miscommunication. When John and I moved from Belize to Grenada for his job, I didn't make my intentions or fears clear. I had a lot of mixed emotions about the move that I stuffed down and kept to myself. In the end, I silently blamed him for how miserable my life had become in this strange new place. Was it his fault? Not really. I was the one who didn't take the time to communicate my feelings to him at a time when we could have made a different decision.

It was extremely unfair on my part because I know that he did the best he could, but I really did not want to move from Belize. So, I held onto what I had there, refusing to let go and make room for what possibilities Grenada might have held. If I had communicated openly and honestly about the move from the start, we could have made different arrangements or come to a compromise that we both felt good about.

Each of you being clear on the "why" behind your decisions as a couple is important. Once you come to a place of understanding, whatever decisions or plans you make come from a place of clarity and mutual agreement. For your marriage to work, you must see both of you in the big decisions; you must see family and the duality of your lives, but you must also see yourself. Make time to spend with yourself to get crystal clear about your intentions, wants, and needs, and then communicate them with your partner.

Be honest, but also be gentle with yourself. Learn to give yourself grace.

WHERE DID THE FUN GO?

Find the time—make a schedule if it will help—to dedicate a part of your day, even a small part, to just being alone with each other. Have date nights, dance on the patio, listen to each other's fears, dreams, and hopes, and I mean *really* listen. Put your phone in another room. Most importantly, you must *see* your partner. The phrase "I see you" really means "I recognize you; I honor you."

And one more thing: You need to have fun. Sex is another important ingredient in your union, but please, no sex in your big old grandma cotton panties with curlers in your hair and your eyes closed while you focus on the million chores you need to get back to once the deed is done. A friend once told me his wife interrupted sex mid-act to ask, "Did you close the garage door?"

No, no, no!

I want you to think about sex in all its glory, with all the bells and whistles, and even in shades of gray—*all fifty shades*. Life can get in the way, but you can still be spontaneous with your partner.

Date each other once a month by getting dressed up, bringing flowers, and eating at that new place, followed by a make-out session in the car or at home. Think back to when you first met. What were the things that caused the relationship to spark and sizzle? Upgrade them, supersize them, and bring them back to the relationship until you both feel so hot and bothered that not even your miserable old boss will be able to erase the massive grin on your face the next day. Bring back your goosebumps.

SHOULD I TALK ABOUT IT WITH A FRIEND?

Getting advice or blowing off some steam by venting to a friend is fine, and at times, it is necessary. However, I would caution you to think twice about what you say about your romantic relationships and your partner. Issues can be discussed and addressed with friends, but do not go so deep that you're almost forcing treasured friends to disrespect your partner.

This is not the lifeline you need.

The minute you let others wiggle their way in between you and your partner, you lose in all ways possible. In the moment, it might feel good to hear your friend call your significant other a dog or bitch or bastard. A day later, it sounds like an insult you will never forget, and now you hate your friend for saying such a horrible thing. No winning here. Now, you're just mad at everyone.

You can't have effective communication between two parties when you invite in a third one. It often destroys both your relationship and your friendship. The friend can't take it back when things are resolved between the couple. They end up empty-handed, wishing they'd never put their two cents into someone else's relationship.

What can you do during romantic turmoil instead of hitting speed dial to call your best friend? You might need to take a brief pause. Go for a walk. Turn on some loud music. Jump in the tub. Go play with the dog or cat. You will cool down and maybe even realize that your emotions got the better of you in the moment. A friend supporting you will often keep a fight going, because everyone likes drama, and the friend will even unconsciously stoke the fires, bringing up the initial offense again and again.

DON'T BREAK THE TRUST

Once you break the trust, the relationship is over.

Cheating is not the only way to erode the faith you need to maintain the love. There are other situations that can rock your foundation as a couple. For example, you should never weaponize what you learn about the other person. I remember telling my ex-husband about being sexually abused as a child, and that bastard, that unholy son of a gun, later threw it back at me during a quarrel. Our foundation was forever cracked.

Imagine that this is the only person, up to this point, that you have confided in about that horrific experience. You believed in your mutual deep level of trust and consideration. And then—bam! His words turn into a weapon. It felt like my entire insides were ripped out all over again, but ten times worse.

The lesson is to make sure your trust is not misplaced before you hand over your most guarded and vulnerable secrets. In other words, pick the right person. Some people are so wounded that they will do anything to ensure that your wounds are deeper than their wounds. It's crazy to think of the things and people you will put up with when your self-worth is on the rocks.

The key is to not respond to someone out of anger. Even if you see red, part of the trust is protecting your partner *from you*. It's not always the best idea to discuss things when you are mad. Often, you are going to take a tone and a perspective that is very different from the one you would take if you gave yourself some time to cool down.

Of course, one of the biggest ways to erode the trust is cheating. Even the suspicion of that is enough to make serious dents in the relationship.

I remember when things started going downhill in my first marriage. My friends kept telling me that they constantly saw either my or my husband's car at a particular location—and not one I'd ever been to. I even had a client who asked if I lived in that area or had moved there because he'd seen my car there so many times. Man, stuff like that hurts. It really cuts you to the core. Eventually, I told my friends to stop. I didn't want them to tell me anything. You can't help it; sometimes you do blame the messenger.

"If I have to know, I will find out on my own," I said.

It's hard enough to admit to hard truths, but it's even more difficult to discover them through others. In addition to the pain of betrayal, there is the wince of embarrassment and feeling like a total fool because others know more about what is really going on in your love life than you do. You can tell in their downcast eyes and uneasy vocal tones. Some of the worst aspects of betrayal are others letting you in on a secret that will forever haunt your days and nights.

I longed to discover the sad things for myself before anyone could bring them to my attention. One night, while driving my friend in her car to visit my best friend who was moving the following day, I took an unusual route. Lo and behold, there was my car, parked exactly where others had warned me I'd find it.

Oddly, a sense of calm came over me. I didn't know that I possessed such strength, but I pulled over and told my friend, "I need to collect something."

Impassively, I walked through the gate leading to the house and knocked on the door of the home where my car was parked. I had no idea who lived there, but I wasn't surprised when a woman answered.

"Who is it?" she called out. I knew instantly whom that voice belonged to because I had heard that voice too many times at family gatherings.

"It's Judy," I said.

Boy, oh boy, did I wish in that instant that I was a fly on the wall inside the house. It was so quiet in there that you could hear a pin drop. The element of shock was obviously quite effective, as it took them several minutes to make the next move. Standing outside the door, I calmly waited for a while before knocking again.

"Just to remind you," I said, "I'm still out here."

Brian was the one to emerge, and the look on his face was priceless. Proving that time does indeed heal all wounds, I'm actually laughing as I write this portion of the book.

What I remember from this "confrontation" is that I was so cool and collected. I would not show them one ounce of anger or sadness. In fact, I gave my dear husband the biggest smile I could muster—a 10.0 Olympian effort.

"Well," I said, "I guess you can't blame anyone for telling me now. I've seen it with my own eyes. And, by the way, could you please take my car home and come back with your own?"

He was dumbfounded as I turned on my heels and walked back to the car where my best friend was waiting. I didn't say a word to her about what had just transpired. I would tell her long after the fact, but that night wasn't the right time. I swung the car around, and we drove to the nightclub and had a really great time. Somehow, I kept my composure and looked as carefree as possible. Underneath that composure, I was a wreck inside. That shit hurt as badly as you can imagine, but the tears would have to wait until I was alone. I had promised my friend a night out, and at least someone could keep their promise that night.

As I had a few drinks and even danced, I was numb inside, which was preferable to a brief period where crazy thoughts ran through my head. I was a woman, so clearly it was my fault. Somehow. Some way. Clearly, I had not been a good wife. What was missing inside of me or outside that made him cheat? Another drink. Evil thoughts emerged, as they do when Kool & the Gang insist that you celebrate good times. *I'll celebrate all right, by killing him and getting away with it!* I wasn't really going to do it, of course, but it felt good to dip a toe into the vengeance pool by thinking it.

It's sad that, as women, we often blame ourselves when the trust is broken with our partner. Interestingly enough, I didn't blame the other woman or want to take it out on her. I was lucid enough to know that he was supposed to know and respect the fact that he was a married man. He was the one who should have known the damage he was doing to our marriage. He was the one who had made a commitment to me and had spoken vows declaring a future dedicated to faithfulness and love. He was the one who had betrayed those promises.

Confession: It took me a long time to let go of the anger bubbling under the surface and to be able to look at him without murderous thoughts.

In the weeks that followed, our home was as cold and quiet as a graveyard, which was appropriate because the end of a relationship is a death. I did not bring up the incident, and he was scared shitless to broach the subject. I simply continued doing the things I would normally do: go to work, cook, wash the clothes, and watch TV. I was all about the normal mundane house duties. My contemplative composure was a strength I did not know I possessed. It was driving him nuts, as I think he wanted me to have a screaming fit. But this worked even better on his psyche.

One day, he just couldn't deal with the quiet or my behavior any longer.

Mentally, he snapped.

"Well at least curse me, nah," he said.

I gave him a very puzzled look and asked, "Why, did you do something?"

ADMIT THE TRUTH

That was the end of the conversation for me because, mentally, I had already checked out. I remember when I called my mother to tell her that we had separated, she said to me, "I knew that would happen." I was taken aback, so I asked her why she didn't tell me not to marry him. My mother is a very wise woman, as is evidenced by the question that followed.

"If I had said that to you when you were about to get married, would you have listened?" she asked.

Mom always had a way to get to the heart of the matter. Though I would have hated to admit it, she was probably correct. I would have gone through with it just because she told me *not* to do it, especially at that young age when rebellion was so delicious.

Remember when I told you not to let others force the trajectory of your life? Well, we also have to be careful not to allow ourselves to force it in one direction over another out of our stubborn desire to prove someone wrong. I know this seems like something that shouldn't even need to be said because it's common sense, right? But I've learned how quickly common sense can go out the window under the right or wrong circumstances, depending on how you look at it.

UNFILTERED:

All the signs are usually there in our faces. Take the time to look closely at your choices instead of choosing to turn a blind eye to the truth.

Unfortunately, most times when we think we are in love, we see only what we want to see and block out what we see as undesirable. The problem is that this strategy almost always works against us.

A WORD ABOUT ABUSE

As you begin to audit your relationships to question whether they are right for you, please understand that your decision to refuse to accept abuse in your life should be holistic. I am asking you to please remember that abuse is not just physical. Emotional abuse is abuse, financial abuse is abuse, and none of it should be tolerated.

If you find yourself in an abusive relationship, please seek help. Now. No one deserves to stay stuck in a cycle of abuse. You deserve better. Getting help to remove yourself from an abusive situation is a crucial first step in your journey to recovery. You need to save your own life.

I hope you're fortunate enough to never know abuse and to have the strength to stop abuse from happening to others. This often starts with ourselves, however much we hate to admit it. Consider how you might be exhibiting abusive behaviors, even if it's done unknowingly or unintentionally. Hurt people tend to hurt other people. Pain leads to perpetuating the very cycles we wish to break. So, ask yourself if your first reaction to an uncomfortable situation is to get defensive or to be abusive with your words or deeds. Let's learn to sit with the situation and the feelings before we react with nasty talk or emotional abuse.

In doing the inner work to adjust my mindset to a higher frequency, I've learned to respond rather than react. I hold my power and refuse to give it away.

UNAPOLOGETIC:

It is actually badass to curb your own temper, to think about your words, and to not lash out in anger—even if you're hurting.

FORGIVENESS IS POSSIBLE

Forgiveness goes a long, long way in a relationship. We'll talk more about forgiveness in chapter eleven, but again, I'm not suggesting you forgive him seventy times for the same you-know-what, though we are all fallible and deserving of mercy in certain situations. Never forgive abuse, but other relationship roadblocks can receive your mercy on a case-by-case basis.

Sometimes, therapy helps as you struggle with past demons. If you claim to forgive but continue to hold a grudge in your heart, you are not *really* forgiving. When old issues surface, take a breath and remember why you chose to let them go. Ask yourself if holding on to the hurt is serving you somehow. But if you are in physical or emotional danger, take forgiveness off the table and never turn back.

STARTING OVER

One last thing …

All of us have our drama and baggage. *We all do.* So, when you leave one partner, know that the next will also come with their own fair share.

It's just a matter of proportion. You need to make the decision for yourself who is worth fighting for and what is worth working through.

Rest assured that there will always be things to work through, whether you settle down with a movie star or your average Joe.

And if you do decide to move on, congratulations! It may not feel like it at the time, but taking ownership of your life is always worth celebrating. You will find love and joy again, and your next partner should consider themselves very lucky.

A CONVERSATION WITH YOURSELF

Stop telling yourself:

- I must settle because nothing better will come.

- I must sacrifice myself to keep love, even enduring abuse.

- Others know what's best for my relationship.

Start telling yourself:

- Love doesn't have to define me.

- I matter equally in every relationship.

- Love is work, but also big, sexy, wonderful fun.

NOTES
FOR YOUR JOURNEY

CHAPTER SEVEN
When Things Fall Apart

We talk about "falling" in love—not walking, skipping, or easing into it. Why falling? Because love hits hard. When you reach its destination, it knocks you straight onto your ass.

Sometimes, that love is equally reciprocated and you can soak it in together. Other times, what you receive back is so far from love it might as well be as far as east from west. But that doesn't make *your* feelings any less real, and that can be a difficult road to navigate.

I think people get it wrong when they imply that if we were not loved in return, it wasn't real love. It may be true that it wasn't love for your partner, but that doesn't mean it wasn't real for you—a difference I feel it is important to note.

We are all human: imperfect, flawed, and sometimes a little crazy. We mess up, make mistakes, and can act a fool over things that don't even make sense. Despite our best efforts, things just don't work out sometimes, and we have to get up, dust ourselves off, and move along. Even in the best relationships, there will be pain at some point. That's life, and that's relationships. That's love.

Often, when relationships end, it hurts like hell, and you want to make the monster responsible for breaking your heart pay. You want to make them suffer for all the anguish you are enduring, for all the life that you have missed while focusing on your relationship, and for all the sacrifices you made for them. But choosing to stay stuck in hate and wanting them to pay for your pain is, as they say, like drinking poison and expecting someone else to die.

YOU FEAR THE END IS NEAR

When my first marriage ended, I went through a myriad of emotions. Some of them I still don't understand twenty-plus years later. However, what I do know is that if I journeyed back to the beginning of that relationship, it would now be clear as day to see how it was all going to end.

Do you know the song, "Love Don't Live Here Anymore"? It seems, from interpretation, that the singer thought love had abandoned her, and may I dare say that is how most of us process our hurt after a relationship has ended. Depending on the relationship, getting past that hurt sometimes feels impossible.

I once had a boyfriend from whom I was inseparable for a while. My friends were upset with me because I no longer wanted to spend time with them the way I had before. That time was now solely devoted to my relationship. When we broke up, it was a huge deal. I was pretty lucky that my friends came back to help me deal with the fallout of that relationship ending. I still think it was the most hurtful breakup that I've ever experienced.

Why? Because he was the one who left.

My ego was shattered to bits because, up to that point, I'd always done the leaving in any relationship I had been in. So, I wasn't hurt that the relationship had ended, but I *was* hurt that *I* didn't get to leave first. My hurt was all driven by ego—plain and simple.

DIFFERENT BREAKUPS, DIFFERENT PAIN

We all handle the death of relationships differently.

One woman I knew lived with her partner for twenty-five years, though he remained married to another. When he died suddenly, his wife—legally entitled to everything—stripped his partner bare. Twenty-five years of unhealed pain had festered until the wife's only thought was revenge.

Was she legally entitled to her husband's estate? Yes. Could she have gone about things differently? Absolutely. When the ego rules, it prevents us from leading with love and compassion.

I know another woman who lived with her lover for thirty-five years. This is such an ill-fated story that it makes me wonder what causes love to turn to such bitter hate. Was it even love in the first place? This relationship was doomed from the very beginning. When she was pregnant with their first child, another woman was also pregnant by him. He was having two first babies at the same time. This is the reality for many women in the Caribbean.

My father has several families. I am quite sure that I have siblings whom I've never met. The thing is, many women choose to remain in those relationships, and I use the word *choose* loosely here, because when we are in an unconscious state—when we are ruled by our egos—I am not too sure there is a choice. We do what's familiar to us, even if that familiarity means more pain.

In his book *The Power of Now*, Eckhart Tolle says that the mind always adheres to the known. When we stay in any relationship built on disrespect and despair, the result is that we are each so full of pain that we end up woefully spiteful and want to hurt the very person we loved at the start.

Is it really possible for love to turn to such bitter hatred? The answer is yes. My friend in the thirty-five-year relationship now spends her life just looking for ways to make the man's existence a living hell. She stalks his apartment, follows him around town, calls his new girlfriend, and wakes them up in the middle of the night with endless texting.

In breakups, I believe that the pain becomes our default. It's comfortable because it's familiar, and we fear what lies beyond it: the unknown. Even though it promises something deeper and far greater than the pain we are currently experiencing, it is uncharted territory, and that scares us more than staying in our misfortune, so we fail to embrace it.

One of the worst ways a romance can end is if either party is cheating. We jokingly say that Caribbean men "have the right to cheat." It's almost as if cheating is the favorite pastime of our men. History is littered with tales of adulterous relationships. Some have stood the test of time, while others have ended disastrously. The point is that infidelity and affairs are not new and have been going on since the beginning of time. Some of these legendary affairs have even helped to shape history.

We just don't want them to shape *our* history, because it hurts when they do.

CAN YOU FALL OUT OF LOVE?

I don't believe that people fall out of love. I believe we enter different phases of our lives, and sometimes, we do so without being in tandem with each other. If we are not aware that we are moving in opposite directions or that we are not in sync, then things will go awry. I also believe if one of the parties in the relationship wants to go, the best thing the other person can do is to let them walk right out that door.

After you have done all you can do—including going to counseling—if your partner still wants to go, let them go. The worst thing you can do to yourself, and to your partner, is force them into something they don't want. Believe me, I know how their desire to leave hurts. I know that pain all too well. Take comfort in the fact that nothing lasts forever. Nothing ever remains the same. This too shall pass. The hurt will go away, and you will come out stronger on the other side.

My friend Khadine is quite clever in describing how she sees, feels, and thinks about a breakup, calling it "a necessary ending and a necessary evil." I agree, and it's frankly how I view and treat any breakup. Whether it's a friendship that is no longer serving a good purpose and has become toxic or a romantic endeavor that has expired and run its course, we all know when it's time to make a hard call and extract ourselves from that situation.

Khadine broke it down for me:

"For me, the decision is quite easy sometimes, and the execution of it may be also. Yes, I know that sounds cold as hell, but based on who and what, it needs to be a quick and a clean-cut break. Know that every person we encounter, and every man that we meet, like, and think that we are head-over-heels in love with is not meant to be around us or with us for a lifetime."

How does she know when to pull the romance plug? "When I begin feeling more upset around someone than I do happy, then it's time for that cut. If their presence causes me anguish, anxiety, or anger, more often than not, then it's time," she says, adding:

"If you no longer show me respect and do not value my feelings and opinions, then it's time. If we have different goals, dreams, and intentions for ourselves and for each other, and they do not and cannot be merged or compromised on, it's time. If we have interests in other people, well, hell yeah, it's absolutely, positively, about past that time. Let's have that dreaded conversation and go our separate ways."

Let's not resist who we are in exchange for a counterfeit version. Learn to remove yourself from situations and people who do not serve you on a higher level and whom you cannot serve on a higher level. Learn to appreciate who you are, fully and without judgment, so that you can enjoy a life filled with love, joy, and peace. Learn the art of walking away.

This change may mean that you might need to make some adjustments to your lifestyle. Whatever you do, do not make the mistake of staying in a relationship for the lifestyle. You are much more than a lifestyle. Do not attach the label of "hopeless" to yourself if you don't have that lifestyle.

UNFILTERED:

Don't make the leaving mean and nasty. Don't try to make someone else pay. Remember that you want to send out the vibrations that you wish to receive in return.

DEALING WITH DIVORCE

The pain of divorce is especially hard, even if it's a relationship you never really wanted. When my first marriage ended, it was painful, even though I knew, all along, that it needed to come to an end. But the circumstances in which it ended made it even more painful. Sometimes, we mastermind our own hurt. I knew that the relationship was doomed from the start, but I talked myself into thinking that if I had a child, it would fix the situation—as if a child is a problem solver.

As I told you earlier, when I announced to Brian that maybe having a child would solve our issues, he told me that I was not mentally ready. So, you could imagine my devastation when I found out that another woman was pregnant with his child.

I remember when my mother was pregnant with my last brother, some forty-odd years ago, she told my father that his time was up and he was not welcome in her home anymore. They were not married, and it couldn't have been easy for her in that moment. My father always had several families he would fluctuate between, so I suffered from "daddy issues" for quite a while, and I gravitated toward relationships I believed could fill that void.

When Brian and I finally broke it off, I still had to face the fact that, "*Shit!* This really is over." I kid you not, I stayed in bed for a whole week, only getting up once to shower. I felt like a total failure. All those fucked up thoughts kept swirling around in my head. I kept telling myself I wasn't good enough. In my mind, there was so much shit wrong with me that I couldn't even manage to keep my husband. *If only I had gotten pregnant, things would have been better.* I know *now* that sort of thinking is just foolish, but it was how I felt at the time, in my moment of extreme pain.

You know how they say the best way to get out is to go through it? Well, my brother Kevin and my friends helped me get through. I remember Kevin coming into my room, throwing open the windows, pulling back the curtains, and telling me that I needed to get up and take a shower because I stank. *All true!*

My friends went to battle for me, fighting every single negative thought I had. They challenged my faulty thinking, listing out loud every good attribute I possessed. They didn't cease until I believed in myself again. That's when I realized that we stay in bad relationships because we're seeking validation from someone else. *Bam! There it is!*

As for my story, I had to face some hard facts. The woman my husband was cheating on me with was someone who was always at family gatherings. Her uncle was married to Brian's aunt, who'd raised him. To make matters worse, she was *also* married at the time. When I found out, the pain was multiplied because she was someone I considered family, and *Man, family doesn't do that sort of thing to one another.* Well, that was my thinking at the time.

I knew that marriage had to end, but I kept putting off having the conversation. That's what we do when a conversation is especially difficult. We put off for tomorrow what should be done today. We worry about how we are going to get by, how we are going to pay the rent or the mortgage by ourselves, but most of all, we are deathly afraid of being alone.

I had to spend some solo time in deep thought. The end result was stunning. When we get comfortable with ourselves, when we get to the point where we know who we are and recognize the things that no longer serve us, it becomes easier for us to walk away from toxic relationships and people.

I had to learn to fly on my own.

UNFILTERED:

Alone gives you the time to figure it out.

HOW TO FLY SOLO

People treat singleness like it's a disease. The thought is that it's somehow better to be in a relationship full of negative side effects than to be single. This is exactly the type of thought that has us jumping into and staying in relationships that we have no business being in.

Take the time to be on your own. Go to the movies by yourself, buy yourself flowers just because you love the smell and looking at them brightens your day. Treat yourself and get to a place where you are content being alone because, in reality, you don't *need* a relationship to make you happy or whole. You *want* a relationship, and good relationships are nice to have in life, but not having one is not the end of the world. And chances are, if you feel unhappy or dissatisfied with life outside of a relationship, then being in one is not going to fix that.

During and after my divorce, I asked myself, *Why did it have to take this horrific experience for me to wise up?* I knew from the onset that the relationship was not the right one for me, yet I persisted and stayed. I told myself I was not good enough to be loved and appreciated. I remember remarking to my friend one day that I would lose weight, and then Brian would want me. She gazed at me with a puzzled look on her face and asked me why I didn't lose the weight for me. *Why did I think that I had to do it for him? What about me?*

I believe a lot of what we go through on a psychological level as women is based on how we are socialized. Even though I went through what I considered a rather traumatic experience, I still felt that to be complete, I needed someone.

It took several years of going through what I call a smiling depression and being reduced to nothing mentally for me to have that very hard, much-needed conversation with myself about the direction I wanted my life to take. I had to make some tough decisions to reach the point where I could look in the mirror, smile, and say, "You are one smart, together, unapologetic, and yes, hot chick." It was hard, but it was so worth it.

UNFILTERED:

What conversations are you having with yourself that keep you in that dead-end marriage, where you don't speak to each other at home but you put on a show in public? What conversations are keeping you in a relationship where each of you is living a separate life, but you stay with each other because you have a house, a car, and some kids? What about you?

IS THIS A GIRL THING?

Too often, we gossip about divorced sisters instead of supporting them, hurting our collective cause. We have been brainwashed to think we are in competition with each other. No, we're not! There are enough men to go around. There is enough of everything that we think is scarce. By supporting each other, no one loses and everyone wins.

Sisters, we must stop competing with each other and tearing each other down. We are better than that. This is a conversation we need to have with ourselves *and* with each other.

UNFILTERED:

What's going to be the conversation you have with your Maker when you finally meet face-to-face? Know that the quality of that conversation depends heavily on the conversations you are having with yourself. Make it a damn good one.

When I was in my early twenties, I met one of the most amazing women ever. We started talking, and I learned that she had gone through one hell of a divorce. Her husband was abusive, even though she was the one bringing home the bacon, frying it, *and* cleaning up after it. She was super talented, and after she got the courage to leave the marriage, her life began to lift off and reach new levels. She started her own business and became very successful.

All it takes is for you to find that courage within yourself and find a great support system. I have always been a support to my friend, just as she has been to me, and I won't ever stop. By support, I mean listening, talking, watching a movie together, eating a meal, sitting in silence, taking a hike, or whatever it takes to be there for another human being.

EMBRACE JUST BEING

After a divorce or split, it's helpful to use the time alone to get to know yourself all over again. Work on you—upgrade your skills, acquire new ones, but whatever you do, don't lie down defeated. Take a day or two (or three) to wallow, if you must, and then get up and get going. You are stronger, wiser, and more resilient than you know. And remember those girlfriends? Your tribe? Call them in to ride out this storm with you. They've been exactly where you are now.

Embrace the change and the newness of being single. Your determination and your tribe's support will carry you through anything. Know that goodness is waiting for you on the other side.

Above all, keep the faith.

A CONVERSATION WITH YOURSELF

Stop telling yourself:

- It's all my fault.

- I will never meet anyone again.

- I am washed up.

Start telling yourself:

- My mistakes don't define me.

- I am hot shit (and then some!).

- My tribe's got this.

NOTES
FOR YOUR JOURNEY

CHAPTER EIGHT
Friendship

When I think about friendship, I think about my siblings—built-in friends who shared all our memories, hopes, and dreams. My closest friend, then and now, is my brother Elwyn. We were born three years apart and were always together. Every night, as we lay on our sponge mattress on the floor of our one-bedroom house, he'd ask about my imaginary friend, Tarlie. "What did Tarlie do today?" he'd ask after lights out, and I'd spin tales of Tarlie's wisdom and adventures. Elwyn never dismissed these stories as childish; he encouraged my creativity before I even knew that word. In the morning, Elwyn would comb my long hair before school. He knew of only one hairstyle: one part in the front and two parts at the back.

He was my best friend, and we're still close today. Funnily enough, most of my other friends outside of my siblings were the boys in the neighborhood. I related better to the boys than the girls. The girls in those days didn't understand me because I didn't conform to all that "sugar and spice and everything nice." I had no interest in dolls or makeup. Everything was probably just spice in those days.

Why didn't the girls get me? Maybe it was also because I would say the things they were thinking. "Judy, you need to behave yourself," the adults would tell me, followed by "Judy, you need to shut your mouth." My question was, "Why do I have to behave in this particular way?" I'd curse and run around with the boys, which was also off-putting to the girls. Even in those days, I thought, "This is who I am. I don't pretend. I am me."

Boys became my early friends because they accepted me. I did everything they did, including climbing the biggest trees. I would ditch school with them every Friday afternoon. I'd slip away with my friends, and we would go mango picking in the heat or head to the beach. We had no bikes and would make our own toys using old tire rims or bark from trees. Whatever was available was used for our fun. We'd make kites from paper and the "bone" from coconut branches, and our glue was created with flour and water. I was never lacking when I was running with my friends. I look back on those lazy days fondly, and they were complete with laughter, skinned knees, and the ease of that time of my life when I had absolutely no responsibilities.

As time progressed, I built friendships with three girlfriends: the twins, who were actually from the next village over from us, plus one other girl from my own village. After primary school, we all ended up going to different high schools. My godbrother and I were also close. He lived near me but went to a different school. On weekends, we would hang out, and my sister would bake sweet bread. Friends would come over, and we'd sit, talk, and laugh. I've always enjoyed being in the company of friends.

To this day, I love to have great, intellectual conversations. I'm drawn to people, male and female friends, who can provide that kind of mental stimulation. I always lean toward happy people who want to laugh and have fun with each other.

Friendship is one of the great joys of life.

GIRLFRIENDS ARE THE KEY

As I've aged, I've learned nothing compares to the love and support of true friends, especially your girlfriends. No matter how long they stay, girlfriends are an important part of your life. If you grew up with sisters, you know that sisters fight with each other, but behind all that fighting is fierce loyalty. They would defend each other at the drop of a hat. Same with great female friends.

I love that my two daughters are also friends. Yes, they often fight (verbally, not physically), but if I ever punished one, the other would come begging on her behalf. Sometimes, they would even take the blame for each other. They are each other's best friend, and as they grow, my wish is that they remain that way.

MEET MY GIRL SQUAD

My best friend Cherry-Ann has been my friend for more than twenty years and is a true touchstone for me. We met at work and knew instantly we'd be friends forever. Not once during our friendship can I remember us having a disagreement and not talking to one another. Ours is the kind of friendship that is way beyond pettiness. We have our differences, but we have such love and respect for each other that we never allow our differences to affect our friendship negatively. If anything, those differences have helped to strengthen our relationship.

Girlfriends like Cherry-Ann have an uncanny way of being there at just the right time. Recently, I was sitting alone and felt an urge to talk to someone. I started to think about all the people I knew, but I wanted to have a very specific conversation, and I knew none of the people who came to mind could satisfy that conversational need. It was eleven o'clock at night, and there was only one person I could call who would instinctively know what discussion I wanted to have. Cherry-Ann picked up the phone, laughing, as she always is, and without even saying hello, she said, "You called at the right time."

UNFILTERED:

So many times, we think we are alone and have no one to turn to, but we do.

My core set of girlfriends has been in my life for what seems like forever. In fact, I call them my forever friends, and as I am fast approaching my mid-fifties, I have cause to reflect on these friendships. I have known my friend Sallian since I was nineteen. She has gotten me through most of the messes in my life.

As I think about Sallian, my heart is smiling. She has been a staple in my life. At one point, she was my boss, but she was also my friend, and this is something that we managed successfully. She would chew me out for something I did at work, and by five in the evening, we'd be having drinks and laughing at all our stories.

Some people have difficulty separating business and friendship, but that was never a problem for either of us. Thank God for that, because we would have missed out on one heck of a friendship. Where so many people let the spoiled fruit of one area of their life spill over into another, we both understood that there is a balance, and we never held on to temporary grievances.

There is a fine line between friendship and work. On the job, there was a hierarchy, but after hours, we were friends. Our bond has never been broken in over thirty years. She now lives halfway around the world, and we are still as thick as thieves.

When I moved to Belize, Vanessa became another forever friend. Both from Trinidad and Tobago, we formed a natural bond. She'd drop everything to help—like the one day I was bitching and moaning about how difficult it was to look after my two very young children. I have never forgotten her words.

"Please dress my kids. I am coming for them now," she said.

It was a Saturday, which marked her grocery shopping and market day. Vanessa went to the market with my two little ones and her young daughter in tow. It couldn't have been easy, but she sensed from the tone of my voice that I really needed a short break. My friendship with Vanessa is one I do not take lightly and never will.

Relocating far from family tested me. When I first moved to Belize, I was so unhappy that I called my mother daily. Unfortunately, that didn't help one bit because it only made me more homesick, not to mention the hefty phone bills. Gradually, I began to meet people, and I will confess that Belize is the place where I truly grew up. It is home to some of my dearest friends.

It was in Belize that I started celebrating my birthdays. Prior to that, my birthday was never really celebrated, by me or anyone else. Every year, I would cook curry and my friends would bring all the drinks and, of course, a birthday cake. That was our deal. Another thing they insisted on was that the party happened on the day of my birthday (even if it was a Monday). The party started in the middle of the day, and I smile every time I think about it, because everything about those times was so real, so authentic. I still have this image of Karen walking in with a bottle of champagne under each arm and a case of beer in one hand. Those parties were epic!

My Belizean girlfriends taught me the true meaning of friendship. I recall during a grave illness when I was almost at death's door, and my husband and kids had already relocated to another country, these women became my family. One friend came to the hospital nightly, getting into the bed and reading to me until I fell asleep. She would then quietly slip out of the bed and make her way to a chair, where she slept until the following morning. When I needed medical treatment in Florida, another packed her bags before the doctor could even finish speaking. My best friend, Cherry-Ann, turned her study into a bedroom so I could recover with her for three months. My friend Karen flew from Belize to accompany me from Florida to Houston.

I came to truly appreciate the value of the girlfriends I had in my life.

HITTING THE SKIDS

Friendships ebb and flow. When you hit rough patches, clear the air quickly through direct communication. I'm blunt—sometimes, I say things with absolutely no malice that are received poorly. Don't let your mind spiral or resentments build. Most disagreements deserve more than a text—meet in person, share a coffee, make eye contact— as emotions aren't conveyed in a one-sentence electronic message. I've learned that second chances can be valuable; my circle might be larger today if I'd given more of them.

There are some friendships that simply don't last for one reason or another. These are the people who cross your path only because of their intention to help you fail. I've met quite a few of them on my journey. They are the ones who will talk and laugh with you, while at the same time, they are maligning you in a text or WhatsApp message to someone else. They will come to your home, eat with you, and then leave to talk about what you had (and what you didn't) and how it was awful. They will suck the very life out of you and then blame you for allowing it to happen. I have learned to let them go without hurting them or myself. And when you do that, you should have a freaking party!

Before turning forty, I was still living in Belize, and I had this great need to be accepted by the in-crowd. I would do anything to fit in with them. My need for others' acceptance was so great because I hadn't yet accepted myself. The friendships in that circle were so fickle and predicated by social climbing that I remember one acquaintance telling me she was going to stop being friends with one person and establish a friendship with another because the new friend was going to become the wife of the prime minister. It was like living in *The Twilight Zone.* Of course, that's how it is when you live superficially. You rely on superficial things to validate your existence.

I reason that each and every friendship, good or bad, enters our lives for a purpose. Just as you learn and grow from the best friend-ships, you also learn and grow through the bad ones. There is no cause to mourn or even curse as some of these relationships exhaust their usefulness and purpose. Learn to value every lesson, especially the hard ones. Acknowledge your gratitude for the experience and release it from your life.

I am fiercely loyal, so when my trust is betrayed, you don't get a second chance with me. Those relationships are not friendships. Real friendships add value to both lives—anything less is toxic.

Only people who are going through a specific kind of hell use and discard people as if they were trash. Don't let your ego trap you into thinking that you need those types of individuals in your life. Their egos need to be validated, and one way they achieve that is to have you believe that you need them in your life because you're nothing without them. Horseshit!

TELLING YOUR FRIEND THE TRUTH

Friendships with other women—especially and in particular those that are rooted in love and honesty—are important. These are friends who will lovingly kick your ass into gear and encourage you to live as your unfiltered and unapologetic self. These are the friends who will laugh with you, cry with you, and help you bury that metaphorical body. But more than that, we need friends who will hold us accountable. True friends will tell us the hard truths we may not want to hear and will hold us to a much higher standard than we hold ourselves.

All my core friends are like this, but I have one in particular named Eveline, who is a no-holds-barred kind of friend. She's the kind of friend who tells you where you are going wrong and wastes no time mincing her words. She will also let you know when you are on the right track.

Once, I was having an issue in my marriage, and she told me, without restraint, that it was my fault. In her "uppity" Dutch accent, she said that I was "being unreasonable and pigheaded." I was shocked and very upset. She was my friend, and she should side with me, dammit! I'm smiling now because she said to me, "It's precisely *because* I'm your friend that I *am* telling you the truth."

UNFILTERED:

If you have friends who tell you the truth, please cherish them. They are few and far between, and their candid honesty is an absolute asset to your growth as an individual.

I wish I could tell you about all my friends and the importance they have in my life, but time does not permit. I must, however, mention a few more. First, my friend Rita, whom I met for the first time at a party. By the end, we were planning a weekend trip for the following week. Rita and I have a friendship that evolved naturally, and distance would never dilute it. There is also Wendy, who, when I am feeling sorry for myself, finds all the right words to lift my spirits and get me going again. And then there's Luz, who has been a beacon in my leadership journey.

I love all my girlfriends; they have all added value to my life, and I hope that I'm able to do the same for them.

I also have a really good male friend who has forced me to take a hard look at myself. I actually hated him for it at the time. As a matter of fact, I thought all he wanted to do was hurt me. I couldn't have been more wrong. He has taught me to manage my expectations of others. He also encouraged me to reach out to my father after fifteen years of not being in touch. He's the one man I speak to about every issue that's affecting me. He's the first person I call whenever something good or bad happens. We don't see eye to eye on all matters, but it is a friendship that I will always cherish.

IN YOUR CORNER

Your friends should always be in your corner. Even when you are wrong, they should be able to tell you so, all the while remaining close by for support. You want friends who are comfortable coming to your house to cook—friends who, when you are having a bad day, week, or year, know not to ask *if* they should bring wine but *how much* to bring.

We draw strength from our friendships with each other. Our female friends should be our bedrock. We are more confident and beautiful when we have the strong support of our female tribe. Different friends bring different shades and flavors of rich experiences into our lives.

It's important that we get this female friendship thing right because, when we do, magic happens. If you don't have even one friend like this, check out the conversations you are having. Are your mental blocks preventing you from forming deep and lasting bonds? Ask yourself if you are being the right kind of friend to others.

I've been told that to have a friend, I have to first *be* a friend. I guess I've been that friend over the course of my life, and that's why I can now say with certainty that my friends are forever types. These people have kept me standing. They perceive me as a very strong person, and I am. But I'm also human and need the help of friends around me.

Our girlfriends, and indeed all our close friends, are a great source of comfort, joy, confidence, and that warm fuzzy feeling on a Sunday afternoon. To *all* my girlfriends, past and present, I love you. You have added some rich tapestry to my life.

A CONVERSATION WITH YOURSELF

Stop telling yourself:

- Girlfriends are too much drama.

- If I let them in, they might hurt me.

- I'm too tired to be with my friends. (Stop that shit and just go out that front door!)

Start telling yourself:

- I am perfectly imperfect.

- My female tribe is important, and they've got my back.

- I can be vulnerable and strong at the same time.

NOTES
FOR YOUR JOURNEY

CHAPTER NINE

Your Inner Core

When I met my first husband, I was at a stage in life where I got by on how I looked, but deep within, my self-worth was nonexistent, so I was quite happy when he took a fancy to me. Truth be told, I get rather bored with any relationship that does not stimulate me on a higher intellectual level; I believe that I am sapiosexual. My relationship with Brian satisfied my need for self-destruction and intellect, and at that time, my need to self-sabotage and self-destruct was anything but basic. It ran deep—really deep. Every day, the scared little traumatized girl within me controlled every facet of my life, and I needed to destroy every bit of her. The best way I knew how was to drink, smoke, party, and generally live in moral apathy.

Imagine living, as most do, in a self-imposed hell. This may not sit well with religious people, but I believe that we experience heaven and hell based on our belief system. I am also of the view that God is not a man in the sky with a big stick waiting for us to make a mistake so that He can punish us. We are the ones who punish ourselves.

Around that time, I met a very religious lady who was quite different from the norm. She didn't think we would burn in hell for eternity. She believed that the God of the Bible was much more forgiving than popular religious beliefs would have us believe. I grew up in church, like most families in the Caribbean, but primarily because one does not argue with one's mother about going to church. Once I was on my own after school ended, I spent long periods not going. I felt at the time that it held no real meaning for me. But after I met this woman, I started attending a weekly prayer group that she helmed. Even though there was some comfort from those sessions, I had more questions than answers. I kept roaming and searching for something to fill a void that could not be filled by material things or people. I went to various Bible classes and study groups, but the more I attended those events, the more restless I became in life.

Eventually, I just stopped going altogether.

It wasn't until I discovered meditation and, later on, yoga that I began to understand deeper core issues. I believe we keep searching for our purpose and meaning outside ourselves, so much so that we confuse religion and spirituality and use them interchangeably. I have no issues with people and their religions. What I do have an issue with is people hiding behind their religions so that they continue to live in pain. Instead of facing our proverbial demons directly so we can live a life fulfilled, we tend—and this is solely my belief—to misinterpret the parables in the Bible so they fit nicely into our pain.

In my opinion, the Bible is a beautiful book written by men for men, as a sort of moral compass guide. Religion, I believe, is quite performative. It's really a set of institutionalized beliefs, rituals, and practices rooted in the worship of God or a Higher Power. Spirituality, though, I see as being more about a deep connection to a Source bigger than ourselves that allows us to live every single day in gratitude and in a state of constant grace. It is not about going to church every Saturday or Sunday and performing a set of rituals to satisfy the religious codes. Maybe that sounds to you not all that different from organized religion, but trust me: There is a difference here—one we'll talk more about as we move through the chapter. But before we do, you need to hear a little about how I learned to embrace my own spirituality and connect to my Source.

A NEAR-DEATH EXPERIENCE

In 2010, I was at death's door. I went into the hospital for a seemingly routine surgery and ended up spending three months in hospital care in the United States. In the chapter on friendship, I told you about how my friends got me through my illness. Well, now I am going to tell you how my illness got me to my conscious state.

I went for routine surgery, where doctors accidentally nicked my small intestine. I often joke that a roti saved my life. My friend Vanessa, knowing how much I loved her roti, made it for me when I came home after my surgery to stay with her. Since I was not given any instructions when leaving the hospital, I figured any food was fair game. Roti, I now believe, is one of those foods you don't eat after surgery.

I'd dug in, talking and laughing with Vanessa and other friends who came over to visit. Just before I finished eating, I experienced severe stomach pain. I fainted and vomited, scaring shitless my friends who'd just brought me home from the hospital. They managed to clean me up and helped me find a position where I could rest through the pain.

They called the doctor, and I remember asking for her to come with an IV tube and drips because I knew I could not get to the hospital; I was in too much pain to move. The doctor did come with the drips and some painkillers and told my friends to take me to the hospital very early the next day. I was readmitted, and it would take several days before they found the issue.

I was being seen by a different surgeon from the one whom I would later learn caused the problem, but this surgeon insisted on doing only chest x-rays, while my white blood cells kept increasing. He simply refused to do a CT scan, even though I asked for one. *But* (and that's a big but) it pays to have certain types of friends.

A friend came to see me at the hospital and asked me for the gyno's number. When he spoke to her, he simply told her that she was to arrange for me to have a CT scan very early the next morning. She obliged. I remember going through the machine and knowing the exact moment they found the issue. I saw the sudden change in my doctor's expression.

I was airlifted to Cleveland Clinic in Florida that night. By the time I got there, I was extremely weak and in the most excruciating pain. They did further tests while I hovered in and out of consciousness. I can still clearly hear one of the doctors saying, "She needs to be prepped for surgery right away. She has just about twenty-four hours to live."

As I was being wheeled into the theater for surgery, the anesthesiologist looked over my medical chart. As soon as he saw my vitals, he informed the surgeon he would not administer the anesthetic because my readings were already too low.

I'll never forget the surgeon's response.

"You may as well do it. She's dead already," he said.

They thought I could not hear them. I decided there and then that I had two choices. I could use what they said and let it kill my spirit to the point of giving up the fight for life, or I could use it to strengthen my resolve to live. I chose to use it to strengthen my resolve. After ten hours of surgery and recovery, I was joking with the doctors the next day and asked them if they took out the excess fat in my stomach while they were in there. Seven days later, as I was preparing to leave the hospital, one of the nurses came into my room and told me that it was such a pleasure to serve me because I had such a fantastic attitude.

ANSWER FROM YOUR HEART

In that moment, I understood love, I understood friendship, and I understood the value of family. My consciousness shifted to living in the moment.

After searching for and discovering several books on spirituality, I finally understood that your spirituality is not outside of you but that it is deep within. It is your personal relationship with the Universe, with the Supreme Being you identify as God. It is your oneness with creation. I believe that religion puts the onus on your healing outside your purview, while spirituality puts it squarely within you. It is your job to heal yourself, or to at least make the decision to heal.

Growing up and going to church, I was taught that God existed outside of me, somewhere up in the clouds, with a big stick just waiting for me to commit a sin so that He could smack me upside the head or, worse yet, burn my evil ass in eternal damnation. Of course, I know better now. The Universe is loving and always wants what's best for us. I also know that its energy is both feminine and masculine—there are no real words to explain it; I just feel it.

Our spirituality helps us connect the dots. It teaches us that we are all part of something much bigger than ourselves, and that bigger "something" requires us to be kind and gentle to ourselves so we can be kind and gentle to others.

UNFILTERED:

Life is a boomerang. We get back whatever we send out, so we are beholden to sending out the vibes that we want in return.

Even though I'd come far in connecting to my inner being—my "I Am," or my higher self, the part of us that we are disconnected from when we see things as outside ourselves—a void remained until I had a very serendipitous phone call with, oddly enough, a financial coach. She asked me why I didn't have the money I thought I wanted. I was about to give some bullshit answer from my head when she stopped me.

"No, Judy," she said. "Don't answer from your head. Answer from your heart."

That stopped me dead in my tracks. I'd never once thought that anything emotional was holding me back. Didn't I deal with that a long time ago?

At one point in my life, I would go to the supermarket and buy everything, whether I wanted it or not. I did that because food was one of my triggers. But seriously, I went to therapy for that issue and stopped the behavior. Surely it wasn't coming back—or was it?

The financial coach's instruction to answer from my heart instead of my head brought a wave of emotions crashing down, and for the life of me, I could not ignore it any longer. One thing I learned a long time ago is that when my feelings come, I need to let them come and sit with them until I know exactly what they are. So, I sat with the feelings, and let me tell you, all the junk that I'd thought was gone was there in all its stinking glory.

So, I fell into my feelings. I cried and cried and cried, and I journaled and journaled. I poured all my childhood trauma onto those pages, all the disparaging things I felt about myself. I did so feeling that surely all that crap must have been my fault.

I was so tired when I was done that I fell asleep. When I woke up, I felt like a huge load had been lifted off my shoulders, and I could finally think about the past without feeling the immense pain I once experienced. I didn't go back to the past to dwell there; I looked back so I could offer forgiveness to those who hurt me. And that included myself.

All my life, I felt that my father never really saw us. We were there, yes, but he never *truly* saw us. I no longer blame my father for his absence because, as the great Maya Angelou said, "When you know better, you do better."

Now, I smile knowing the healing I needed as it relates to my father will only be achieved through giving and receiving forgiveness. It was not until that experience (becoming fully self-aware, forgiving myself, and releasing him from any and all expectations) that all the books I'd been reading about connecting with your inner self and being present *really* made sense.

I live so consciously now that I experience daily joy and peace like I've never known before. Why? I listen and speak from my heart.

A CAUTIONARY TALE

When I was in the insurance industry in Belize, I met an entrepreneur I truly admired. He seemed to have it all together—a business that looked healthy from the outside and a beautiful family. He also seemed to be a fairly calm soul who never missed church, and he always attended with his family.

One morning, I awoke to the news that he had killed himself in his home, with his family in the adjoining room. Needless to say, I was stunned and devastated at the time. I still feel awful about it. I was also disappointed, not only because the image I'd had was shattered but also because I felt that the church had let him and his family down. I found myself wondering—if religion were more personal and less performative, then would the church brethren have figured out he was troubled? And, if he had embraced his spirituality, would it have let him down as, in my mind, religion had?

This is just me musing in hindsight, but what if he had chosen a different path? What if he'd connected with his inner core and gotten the chance to deal with his demons? Because that's one of the things our shape-shifting egos show up as—demons. When the ego feels threatened, when it feels as if we are about to kill it, it can get to the point where it eats us from the inside out. Getting the help we need is crucial.

Though there have been some strides recently in destigmatizing the negative associations attached to mental health, we still have a long way to go. Everyone processes differently—what works for one person may not work for another. Mental health struggles appear differently in each of us, and there is no one-size-fits-all solution.

Unfortunately, in the Caribbean, we do not take mental health seriously. Fear of being labeled "crazy" keeps us from seeking the help we may desperately need.

UNAPOLOGETIC:

What many fail to realize is that getting help allows us the freedom to connect with our consciousness so we can truly enjoy our lives to the fullest.

When we deny healing, we can't see our beauty or live fully here and now. An unhealed person lives ruminating either on the past or on the future; they don't allow themselves to feel alive in the present moment, and I think that's an unfortunate way to live.

I often think of my nephew Kerwyn, who died at thirty-seven without getting to experience so many of life's wonderful experiences. If he were here now, he would tell me, as he always did, "Judy, today is all you have."

While I miss him dearly, I know he must have been on to something, because he enjoyed every moment of his short life. I learned so much about life and love from that beautiful young man.

ONE CONSCIOUSNESS AND TOTAL FORGIVENESS

I believe there is one consciousness, and you can call it what you will. Some of us call it God, some of us call it Allah, and others Jehovah, but we are all connected through this one consciousness. It brings calm to the chaos in our lives.

There are times when you feel as if you are so stuck. You lose focus and perspective about what is truly important in life. There are times when you feel as if your life is in quicksand; you are sinking, and you feel nothing but helplessness. You don't have the answers, and you don't know where to look for those answers either.

Embracing your true spiritual nature helps to calm the storms and bring clarity and focus of thought. It will produce joy and create the "peace that surpasses all understanding" that the Bible speaks about.

Two of the most important things I've learned through my spiritual journey are self-love and forgiveness. Without forgiveness, we are fucked. It is so important, in fact, that there's an entire chapter dedicated to forgiveness later in the book. For now, I will reiterate what I have already told you: Forgiveness is never for the person you are forgiving; it is always for you. Sit with that for a moment, and as you think about all the hurt you are holding on to, think about how it has destroyed your peace. Let it go. I know it's easier said than done, but trust me on this one—*let it go*. Release the pain and move on.

It is crucial for us to understand that there is no self-love without forgiveness. It's like the instructions on an airplane. You must help yourself before you can help others. You are simply not capable of truly loving or adequately expressing that love for another human being until you have mastered self-love.

I want to encourage you to fully explore and embrace your spiritual nature. Go deep below the surface. There will be moments when you will come face-to-face with your proverbial demons. There are times when you will want to give up and give in, but I promise you that if you only hold on and push through, you will come out victorious.

As you embark on and continue your journey, always remember to be kind to yourself and that our bigger journey consists of a series of unfolding smaller journeys.

Ask yourself what is holding you back from falling into your feelings, so you can get to that place within where there is perfect peace.

A CONVERSATION WITH YOURSELF

Stop telling yourself:

- Unhappiness is my nature, and I can't change it.

- God is punishing me.

- I can't help how I feel.

Start telling yourself:

- I am strong and powerful.

- The present moment is all I have.

- I am forever badass, unfiltered, and unapologetic.

NOTES
FOR YOUR JOURNEY

CHAPTER TEN

Busting Loose

Have you ever seen a caged bird? Do you know why she sings?

Maya Angelou was on to something—I believe she sings because she plans to break free and fly. But sometimes her wings are clipped … maybe even by herself.

Sound familiar?

Women face constant pressure to conform. Work, mother, problem-solve, maintain the house, care for partners, ignore ourselves—repeat daily. Even our sexuality faces judgment, while men are lauded for their sexual prowess.

We are a society of hypocrites who deal in double standards. Every time—and I mean every time—a young girl is "caught" in any kind of sexual activity or what society might consider sexual misconduct, especially if she's with an older and/or married man, she is chastised as you would not believe. And not just by men—you'll hear the worst remarks from other women. But the man is almost never dragged over the coals. Why is that? Why are we enablers of these kinds of distorted conversations and unfair rules?

Answer: Women have always been expected to live by a vastly different set of rules. That makes me crazy because it's the very thing that keeps us stuck in those unhealthy relationships and marriages. If we continue to live our lives based on what other people may or may not think about us, then we will become like the biblical servant who, paralyzed by fear, buried his gift (his "talent," i.e., money—this story comes from Matthew 25:14–30 ESV, the Parable of the Talents) in the ground rather than risk losing it. As women, we hide ourselves and our potential rather than risk judgment or failure.

You will return to your Maker not having truly lived if you don't figure out when to "bust loose." Many women are afraid to even try to live freely. They worry that people will talk. The truth is, no matter what you do, people will talk—so let them.

In the early stages of my friendship with a good friend of mine, he would be afraid to talk to me in public. He was afraid that if people saw us together, they would assume we were having an affair. That kind of thinking frustrated me. At my age and the particular phase where I was in my life, other people's opinions did not concern me. Did I understand where he was coming from? Hell, yes. I understand the dynamics of a very small society, but what I also knew was that those people who would criticize us were probably leading double lives, talking one way and living another.

I live freely by telling myself the following because it's true: I am at a beautiful place in my life, a place filled with peace, love, joy, and blessings. Most of that was created by me.

Is this mantra too self-centered? No. I care deeply for others, but I care more deeply for me. And I do not say this out of selfishness. I say it out of love for myself and others.

UNFILTERED:

You need to give yourself permission to be free in life—free from other people's opinions, views, and expectations. The truth is that most people are too busy living their own lives to be bothered with what you're doing.

SAYING NO ... MORE

The problem is that most women have been raised to be people pleasers. When you are taught to be like this in life, you eventually despise both yourself and the people you are putting yourself aside to please. That's not fair to either of you. I know I'm at a point where I can lovingly say no to a request I do not wish to fulfill. My motto is that if it (whatever it is) does not bring me joy, then I'm not doing it.

Before I started working for myself, I worked in the corporate world. I had a job that was one of the worst ones I had ever held. The culture was toxic, and there were days when that atmosphere would seep into my body and almost threaten to poison me. There were days when I was literally sick at the thought of going into the office. One Friday night, the Universe intervened and gave me the perfect opportunity to bust out.

Hitting the send button on the email with my resignation was one of the most liberating feelings I'd had in a long time. It was an ending but also a beginning. The point is, you are not a prisoner.

UNFILTERED:

In jobs, and even in your relationships, you don't have to stay if it does not serve you.

We lull ourselves into thinking we'll quit that job we hate as soon as the kids get older. And then they do get older, and we find another excuse to stay stuck because we're afraid to move out of our comfort zones. Comfort zones can be dangerous places to linger. Many times, we are blocking our blessings by staying tied to the familiar. Who says a better, more rewarding job isn't waiting for you? Who says the woman or man who can give you the relationship you always wanted isn't just around the corner?

The day I packed my ex-husband's clothes and left them at the door for him, I felt like I'd never felt before. I finally gave myself the permission to be free. Free from letting him convince me that I needed him.

In those moments, don't throw your hands up in the air and convince yourself that your life is over. Don't go to the place that says you will be alone forever. Take a good look in the mirror. You will find the most beautiful, smart, intelligent person you will ever meet. Start a different conversation and give her permission to bust the hell out of her proverbial prison.

SERVE YOURSELF FIRST

One of the tougher lessons I've had to learn in life is not filling up my plate too much. It's hard to feel free when you're overwhelmed.

This is a tough one for me.

Alpha females think we're invincible, fearing disappointment if we ask for help. We want to avoid being seen as a disappointment by showing we are the most capable. We want to excel at it all, on all days, at all hours, no matter if our plate is overflowing onto the floor. We end up taking on a lone-wolf persona, partially because we're working so hard that we end up losing ourselves and our souls. We lose sight of what's important and who we truly are deep down to become the most manic people pleaser.

As long as everyone else is happy, are we happy? The answer is no. We're simply exhausted.

It's crucially important to learn to serve yourself first. Let me tell you, when you keep dipping your bucket to fill up other people's buckets, then yours is eventually empty. The question remains: You've done all these things for other people, but who is filling your bucket?

The answer is to serve yourself first. And the first step is carving out the time. That's why I've dropped everything that does not serve me. I am not sitting on any boards just for the sake of filling a seat. I am not joining any organizations or committees that are not in line with my values. I am not saying yes to things that feel like a no. I know this is hard to do when we believe we are defined by the associations we are part of or when it comes to helping our friends, loved ones, and even almost-strangers.

Take the endless committees, clubs, and groups that many of us are talked into joining. Many people on those boards are not there to actually work, but rather to be seen. Those energies are not what you want in your space as you work on lifting yourself higher.

Recently, I've had cause to reflect on my business life as well. I find that I'm too accessible to people for free business advice. People call me all the time "just to ask a question" or, to put it less delicately, "to pick my brain."

Before I know it, I am helping them reorganize their entire business for free, and the hours are ticking by in a way I don't want to spend them. To be free, one thing you must realize is that your knowledge is a "for fee" service, and you've got to stop giving that energy away for free. Do not feel bad about not giving people (even friends) a free, all-access pass to a knowledge base that took you years to build and hone to perfection. I had to let go of several friendships along my journey to find this new, upgraded, and free me.

Sometimes, freedom also includes reevaluating your personal life. Perhaps you have a friend or partner who is quite controlling. They need to know where you are every minute—who you spoke to that day, what you talked about, and how you spent each second. Freedom might be the only way to save your own life.

There are other times when relationships begin to feel heavy and oppressive. Perhaps you and your partner have grown apart. This can also happen to other close relationships in life, including with siblings and parents. It can be quite sad, but I believe that certain relationships are short stories.

I figure it's this way: People come into your life for a specific reason. After they have fulfilled their purpose, the relationship comes to a natural end. Along my journey, I have had several of these types of relationships. They were there to teach me something profound, but after the lesson was learned, the friendship seemed to die of natural causes.

Don't mourn it. Don't try to cling to it. Set it free. In doing so, you will allow space for something new and better to come in.

The Universe wants to bless you with an abundance of loving relationships, but when you hold on to links you were supposed to free from your world, then your space becomes too crowded. You end up cheating yourself out of some of your deliciousness.

One of my favorite quotes that I'd like to leave you with at the close of this chapter comes from Thich Nhat Hanh, who said, "Letting go gives us freedom, and freedom is the only condition for happiness. If, in our heart, we still cling to anything—anger, anxiety, or possessions—we cannot be free." To be free, truly free, I believe we must also evaluate our relationship with ourselves and start our healing journeys with some self-forgiveness.

A CONVERSATION WITH YOURSELF

Stop telling yourself:

- I am hopeless.

- I am too old.

- I am washed up.

Start telling yourself:

- Hope lives in me.

- I am hot shit (and then some!).

- My tribe's got this.

NOTES
FOR YOUR JOURNEY

CHAPTER ELEVEN

Forgive to Live

There is power in forgiveness. Holding on to hurt is like a kinked water hose—the flow becomes a trickle.

Everything in life is created twice—first in our thoughts, then in the physical. Where your mind goes, your body follows. Whatever is showing up is created by your ruling thoughts.

The starting point of anything is yourself; therefore, forgiveness first starts with you. When we make mistakes, we often beat ourselves up mercilessly, burying the pain and trying to move on. But that does not have to be the way you deal with your mistakes. There is a much better way: Admit that you've made a mistake, own it, correct it, and move on. That sounds simple in theory, but I know it's hard AF in practice. But when we continue this cycle over and over, we end up having so many repressed mistakes that our hose is completely knotted.

The only way you can liberate yourselves from your self-inflicted pain and suffering is to take responsibility and forgive yourself. This means you must forgive and forget the thoughts, decisions, people, or situations that caused the issue in the first place. Forgetting a wrong done to you is one of the hardest acts, especially if you were deeply hurt. It seems almost impossible at times. People often say, "I will forgive, but I will not forget." Then what is the point of forgiving? Holding on to the hurt and not releasing it only serves to restrict your flow of abundance to you. To be truly forgiving, everything must be abolished, including the memory.

I smoked cigarettes for a number of years. I tried several times to stop—I used patches and every other concoction that people told me to try. One Sunday morning, I got up, looked at myself in the mirror, and decided "no more." I smoked the last two cigarettes I had in the pack, and I've never had a desire since that day to smoke again. It's been more than seven years. Most days, I don't even remember that I smoked. What happened? The desire to smoke was gone. True, lasting forgiveness works the same way. When we don't have the thought or idea that causes the action of unforgiveness, then, and only then, can we truly be free.

UNAPOLOGETIC:

The act of forgiveness does not mean that we condone what was done. It simply means we will not respond in ways that keep us in a holding pattern or cause us to be sick.

Speaking of which, did you know it's scientifically proven that practicing forgiveness is good for your health? It can lower the risk of a heart attack, improve your sleep and blood pressure, and reduce feelings of anxiety and depression.[1] We can literally heal ourselves by starting with our thoughts and releasing the things that do not serve us.

---

1   Johns Hopkins Medicine, "Forgiveness: Your Health Depends on It," accessed October 2024, https://www.hopkinsmedicine.org/health/wellness-and-prevention/forgiveness-your-health-depends-on-it

A BEAUTIFUL GARDEN OR CHOKING ON WEEDS

What are the things you need to forgive? What thoughts are you harboring that might be causing you hurt or guilt?

Forgiveness is for your benefit, for your healing. If weeds are allowed to grow in a beautiful garden without being removed, they will eventually choke the flowers and cause them to wither and die.

The same is true of those resentful thoughts you are holding. Those thoughts must be allowed to dissipate into nothingness so only thoughts that serve you can flourish. It becomes unreasonable for us to think we are forgiven if we have not forgiven ourselves. As you begin to release yourself from all your mistakes and less-than-perfect decisions in the past, you are making space for yourself to release those who have wronged you. And this becomes a self-fulfilling prophecy. The more you release yourself, the more you can release others, and the more you can free yourself.

To make space for the abundance you want in your life, you must get rid of the old stuff. If you have an already full closet and you buy more clothes equal to the number you already have in your closet, what do you suppose will happen? That's right. To make space for the new clothes, you must discard the old ones. Unforgiveness keeps us in lack or in poverty consciousness—something we'll talk more about in the upcoming chapter on money.

The thoughts we hold of others are eternal because they exist in our minds. It is all based on the perception of the person, thing, or situation. Therefore, the first thing we must remove from our minds is the thought that people owe us something. What this does is create space for us to start sowing seeds of abundance for those who have wronged us.

This concept of sending thoughts of love, abundance, and expansion to those who have hurt you deeply is a concept your brain will initially reject. It gets better, I promise. As you send out those thoughts of goodness, those thoughts move through you and come back to you. It's a boomerang effect. You are reflecting those same thoughts of goodness and abundance back to yourself.

It is important that we walk the road of forgiveness and understand its cyclical nature. Forgive, and you will be forgiven. This is the simple rule for releasing and allowing yourself to be open to the flow of abundance.

There's even some science to this.[2] You simply cannot expect abundance to flow to you if you're operating at a low vibrational frequency and harboring resentment for yourself or others.

HOW I FORGAVE MYSELF

I've never ever had the chance to live the single life. OK, maybe that is not a totally true statement. I never gave myself the chance to experience what it is to be single: to enjoy living alone, to have breakfast alone, or to go to bed and wake up alone. To have the whole damn bed to myself. For most of my adult life, I felt that I must have someone in my life, and that would account for a greater part of my happiness. Not so. Not true.

The truth is that I've gotten myself into some relationships that caused me more harm than good, and when there was no relationship, there were friends with benefits. Nothing's wrong with that arrangement if that's the life you want to lead; however, I found that it left me feeling empty and unfulfilled.

Afraid to face our inner demons, we seek external fulfillment, forgetting that only we can truly satisfy ourselves. But first, we have

---

2   David Hawkins, *Transcending the Levels of Consciousness* (Hay House, 2015)

to forgive ourselves for the past decisions we have made in life. You must forgive to live.

Where did I get the idea that I could not fly solo?

It was certainly the result of the conditioning I received growing up, where women were taught they needed a man to save them. Caribbean societies take this seriously. They even punish women for choosing to be single. There is so much pressure on women or young girls to eventually get married and have a child, giving their parents those coveted grandbabies.

In my parents' day, things were even worse. Heaven help women if they didn't have a husband and kids. Society wasn't kind to single ladies, casting them as oddities or "old maids." Even now, older women pressure younger ones with, "When will you settle down and have children? When will you have a life?" As if being single is having no life. It's a question that actually pisses me off because I've seen the devastation that rushing to do these things has caused in my life and in the relationships of the women I know.

I know a young woman who even had an actual timeline for when she would marry and then have babies. When the self-imposed time seemed to be running out, she married the first person who came along so she would stay on track with her life goals. Well, I don't have to tell you how much she regrets that decision. She has two kids she loves, but she can't break free from a husband who controls her and allows very little freedom.

UNFILTERED:

We carry these damn Cinderella stories in our heads, wishing and hoping we will get rescued. Why not rescue yourself?

In order to live a satisfying life, I had to choose to give myself permission to be happy—single or married. I acknowledged my need to breathe, to find myself, and to have that all-important relationship with myself before thinking about having a relationship with anyone else. And who knows? When I finally have that deep, intimate relationship with myself—always a work in progress—I may find that's the only relationship I need.

FORGIVE YOURSELF

I've come to realize that the real reason we are afraid of spending time with ourselves is because we have not forgiven ourselves. I've certainly made some mistakes I wish I could undo. One of them, in particular, left me with a great pain in my heart. For a very long time, the guilt I felt about it set me on a path of destruction. I had two abortions, and the shame from that left me guilt-ridden for a long time. Even writing about it now took some deep contemplation because I went back to wondering if society might still judge me.

Fuck it, I finally thought.

My reason for writing this book is not to be bothered about what John or Jane Public thinks but to help women deal with their limiting self-belief systems and finally heal. To that end, I will allow the chips to fall where they may. What I finally figured out back then was that if I wanted any semblance of a life well lived, then I had to forgive myself and move on.

Do I still think about it? Hell, yes. I do. But I also know there's no sense in living in the past. My life includes mothering two of the world's best children, and I'm honored to have been chosen as the mother of my two beautiful girls.

My wish now: I want to be here for them. I want to see them grow from strength to strength. I want to see their journey through life, and to be able to do that, I must live to the fullest expression of who I am. In that way, they can see an example of what it means to enjoy each moment of life.

UNAPOLOGETIC:

You are so much more than your mistakes or your past. You are gunmetal mixed with a little bit of sugar and spice and a touch of nice. You are, my darling, positively unfiltered and can overcome anything.

I am writing all of this for you because I want you to know it's OK. You don't have to be afraid of yourself, your mistakes, or your past. Believe me, I know it's not easy, especially if what happened to you was not your decision—and even if it was your call. I feel your pain, but I know you've got this.

WAYS TO FORGIVE

So, my lovely, look yourself in the mirror or do whatever you need to do to forgive yourself. Here are my favorite Unfiltered and Unapologetic action steps. Remember one thing, ladies: *The value of any principle is in its application.*

STEP ONE: FORGIVING YOURSELF

As I've said—and will continue to say—before we can start to release others, we must first release ourselves. This action step is designed to help you go deep and bring to the surface the things that you need to forgive yourself for.

Get out your journal (you should be accustomed to this by now!) and work through each of these steps:

- Sit quietly in a place where you will be undisturbed.

- Let your thoughts flow back to a situation or a decision you made that causes feelings of anxiety, frustration, or shame when you think about it. List it in your journal. If more than one comes up for you, that's OK. Just list them all.

- Repeat this process as many times as you need to until you can list as many situations as possible. Note: This process is going to cause some discomfort in your body. Don't be alarmed; just sit with those feelings and let your body process them. That is a big part of the healing process.

Answer these questions:

- "Why do I feel hurt, shame, or regret about _____ [choose one of the things that came up for you from the action above]?" Repeat this action with each of the situations that came up.

- "How can I forgive myself and move forward?"

- "What stories am I holding on to about myself that prevent me from taking bold actions in my life? What new stories can I replace them with?"

Finally, once you've processed those stories, write a letter of forgiveness to yourself.

STEP TWO: FORGIVING OTHERS

Forgiveness is a choice you make. You decide. Choosing to forgive someone who has hurt us deeply is one of the hardest acts that we will perform in life. But it is an act that is the most freeing.

Choose someone who has wronged you—you can always start small and work your way up, but do this as many times as necessary to clear and declutter to make space to receive all the goodness possible into your life.

Set the intention to forgive and release that person by bringing into your consciousness all the goodness that came to you from them. Keep this up. Some of the hurt they have caused will certainly come up. As a matter of fact, the hurt may be the first thing that comes up. Don't try to fight it; let it flow. This is where the awareness comes in.

Then, write a release letter to that person, sending them love, compassion, and forgiveness. In the letter, let them know that you forgive and release them from whatever harm they may have caused you—intentionally or unintentionally.

Repeat this process for each person you need to forgive. You don't have to rush this process; take your time. Next, I'll walk you through what to do with these letters.

STEP 3: FIRE RELEASE CEREMONY

A fire release ceremony is the ultimate act of releasing and letting go, as you might recall from the introduction and chapter four. Fire represents cleaning, purification, rebirth, hope, and resurrection. In this case, we are looking for a cleansing and a purification of what is and hope for what can be.

Take the letter of forgiveness you've written to yourself, as well as the letter(s) of release you've written to those you have forgiven, and close the loop by doing a fire releasing ceremony.

Rip both letters into shreds and set them afire, burning them to ashes. Let that release wash over you. Take some deep breaths and release.

The point is to do this for yourself—remember that forgiveness is not a gift you give to others. It's a gift you give to yourself. This action has the powerful energy of bringing closure, and it makes the act of forgiveness complete.

I am proud of you.

UNFILTERED:

Love yourself fifty ways 'til Sunday, baby girl. Stand up, and then you can stand in love with someone else.

A CONVERSATION WITH YOURSELF

Stop telling yourself:

- My past is too complicated and bad.

- I am broken and beyond repair.

- I can never forgive myself.

Start telling yourself:

- I am a conqueror.

- I love you and forgive you, gorgeous.

- I embrace your badass single self.

NOTES
FOR YOUR JOURNEY

CHAPTER TWELVE

You and Your Money

Money is such an emotionally charged subject—many women prefer not to deal with it at all, inheriting our parents' money attitudes instead. If you grew up around constant arguments about money, then having money might make you nervous and unconsciously send it away. In the Caribbean, we heard "money is the root of all evil," and that "it's easier for a camel to go through the eyes of a needle than for a rich man to enter heaven." Thank God I'm not a man—I intend to be wealthy and still enter the kingdom of heaven. Besides, it's easier to cry in a Mercedes than it is to cry on a bicycle.

Sadly, many women hope their partners will be financial saviors, not because they can't make their own money but because they're taught to leave finances to men. Then, they end up broke when he makes shady investments with their retirement savings.

UNFILTERED:

Know what's happening with your finances. Don't leave it to others.

In many cultures, money is a social status symbol. We sink ourselves deeper and deeper into debt just so we can fucking keep up with the Joneses—whoever they are—with big houses and expensive cars. What I've found is that our need to spend to impress is directly linked to our feelings of self-worth. We think we are not good enough, so we need the next hot, trendy thing that comes along to make ourselves worthy. Just know that the next new "thingy" won't help your self-worth. Needless spending will just ensure that you keep falling deeper and deeper into debt. A scarcity mindset blinds us to existing abundance. We continually see life through the lens of the things we don't have rather than what we do have. I believe I create my reality. It does not matter what my current situation looks like because I can change it with the thoughts I hold and the actions I take.

There is so much information available about money and finances at the click of a button now. You can seek out that which will put you on a path of growth. One thing we must always remember is that, on average, women live longer than men. So, at some point in our lives, we must plan on being alone, even if we are married or partnered. The world has changed and is in a constant state of flux, so retirement does not have to look like your parents' or grandparents' golden years. The one thing you must do is plan for it.

WOMEN: A HISTORY WITH MONEY

As girls, we were socialized to not toot our own horns. Keep silent. Speak only when spoken to. Do not speak up for yourself. Does that sound familiar? We take this baggage and bring it into our adult lives, and it invades our work lives, too. It significantly affects our purses. We do not negotiate our salaries and tend mostly to accept what is being offered. This happens even when we know we are smarter than all the men in the room. We allow ourselves to be bullied and even overlooked for promotions. And we remain silent.

Sex and the City author Candace Bushnell once wrote, "Women with money and women in power are two uncomfortable ideas in our society."

Sure, we talk about money, jobs, promotions, and even lack of funding in our sister circle, but we don't address it head on. We'll complain we don't have enough, our bosses are unfair and don't pay us our worth, and we work too much for too little pay. Girls, we don't take enough responsibility by admitting: I never asked for that raise. I accepted that low offer. I don't dare ask for more money because I'm afraid of being let go.

The truth is that not having enough money or the knowledge to help us acquire that money significantly hinders us from moving forward in life. Most women, sadly, work either unpaid or underpaid. Women make 81 cents on the dollar compared to men, and for Black women, it's less—around 65 to 58 cents.[3] Given that fact, if you're not even *asking* for more money, it's worse.

Sisters, life begins when you take control and ask for what you deserve. Ask for that raise. Demand that promotion. We are now in a time where women are more educated, more active, and much more influential. There are more independently wealthy women than at any other time in history. Women are heading corporations in industries that were usually male dominated. Women also have tremendous

---

3   Elise Gould, Jessica Schieder, and Kathleen Geier, "What is the gender pay gap and is it real?" Economic Policy Institute, October 20, 2016, accessed October 2024, https://www.epi.org/publication/what-is-the-gender-pay-gap-and-is-it-real/

purchasing power—over 80 percent of purchases are made or influenced by women.[4]

We have come a long way and are still going—no stopping us now. Age truly is just a number, and you can rock it into your fifties and sixties … all the way up into your nineties (and maybe hundreds, if you are so lucky!). Don't let beauty magazines define you as over the hill. Women still have tremendous earning power into the older decades of their lives.

THE FUTURE OF YOUR MONEY

As you step boldly into your future, remember the following:

- Plan for retirement now, whether you expect to keep working or not. Save and invest while living in the moment. Prioritize your health, too—it saves money and enriches your life. I took small steps: Cutting back on meat lowered my cholesterol, and quitting smoking brought back my pink lips.

- Never think you're too old to pursue dreams. Start where you are and center your life around your passions—they might even generate income while making learning feel effortless.

- Live mindfully, letting go of past regrets to protect your mental and financial health. Trust your experience to guide sound money decisions. Choose happiness by keeping energy vampires at a distance and negative thoughts at bay.

---

4   Rebecca Betterton, "The rising purchasing power of women: Facts and statistics," Bankrate, January 4, 2023, accessed October 2024, https://www.bankrate.com/loans/personal-loans/purchasing-power-of-women-statistics/

- Most importantly, make peace with money. Form a relationship with it regardless of how much you have. Think abundance, not scarcity—the latter is always an illusion. Be blessed.

A CONVERSATION WITH YOURSELF

Stop telling yourself:

- Money is evil and scarce.

- I am terrible with money.

- Success will cost me relationships.

Start telling yourself:

- Money is energy and opportunity.

- I have a great relationship with my money.

- There is more than enough for everyone.

NOTES
FOR YOUR JOURNEY

CHAPTER THIRTEEN

Grace Through Gratitude

I believe gratitude is an inside job and you get to gratitude through grace. Giving grace to yourself and others is the way. When we are in a state of unawareness, we go through life seeing the glass as having nothing in it when, in fact, the glass already has all we need. The problem is that we love looking at life through other people's lenses, and that can make us either bitter or better. It is especially important that we remain in gratitude and give ourselves some grace, even for the things we think we should have but don't. During much of my search for the meaning of this thing called life, I have discovered that gratitude is my tipping point to abundance. I've also discovered that there are different types of gratitude.

There's conditional gratitude—being grateful only when something specific happens—and there's being grateful *for* specific things and people. But the most powerful is being grateful *in* all things, regardless of what mountains lie in your path. This gratitude, coming from our core, puts us in the driver's seat of our lives. It's generative, giving life to our dreams, goals, and visions.

All the world's traditional wisdom emphasizes the importance of gratitude. It has been around since forever. Having gratitude in all things increases the abundance in your life.

Now, I fully understand how hard it is to be grateful when you think your life is falling apart and you can't see a path through. For example, maybe you've lost a loved one to illness, and you're wondering how you can be grateful at such a time.

We are very happy when things are going great in our lives, and it's easy for us to be grateful. But when things are at their hardest, we must continue our gratitude practice. Every morning, I get up at 4:30 a.m. Before my feet hit the ground, I say thank you. Then, I exercise—either running or going to the gym—followed by a shower, gratitude prayer, and meditation. These three practices set me up to take on whatever comes my way during the day.

Gratitude is a choice, and the more we choose to be grateful, the more we have to be grateful for in life. When we live from gratitude, our eyes open to opportunities that are in front of us, but we can't see them from a position of lack, doubt, fear, and worry. My best advice? Remain *in* gratitude, always.

HOW TO PRACTICE GRATITUDE

We explored forgiveness in a previous chapter—one step toward gratitude is practicing the art of forgiveness. The only way you can liberate yourself from your self-inflicted pain and suffering—to be able to live *in* gratitude—is to take responsibility and forgive yourself, and then to forgive and forget the wrongs that have been done to you. Only then, having released the hurt, can you allow abundance and gratitude to flow through you. Because I have learned to forgive myself, to hold grace for myself when making hard decisions or mistakes, I have found the deepest gratitude, especially for my two girls—my two blessings who arrived at the exact right time they were meant to.

It is important that we walk the road of forgiveness to get to gratitude through grace. It is important that we understand the cyclical nature of forgiveness. Forgive, and you will be forgiven. This is the simple rule for releasing and allowing yourself to be open to the flow of abundance through gratitude.

In the earlier chapter on forgiveness, I had you go through some exercises, writing letters to yourself and others to release the hurt you carry in a fire release ceremony. I'll ask you to do something similar in this chapter, but this time, we're not burning anything. When you wrote the letters, you were naming your deepest fears, worries, and anxieties. Writing them down with pen and paper (as I will always recommend, even if it makes me old-fashioned) provides something cathartic. Writing down what you're grateful for has a similar effect. Take a few moments to journal about this—don't stop until you've filled at least one complete page. This practice brings you closer to the present moment, allowing you to live within it more fully because now you're living *within gratitude*.

UNFILTERED:

We have to learn to release our trauma. The more we try to suppress it, the more it wants to be seen. Bringing light to the darkness and remaining in gratitude, no matter what is happening, is truly something to behold.

This is a profound exercise because once you've released your hurt, found forgiveness, and started living within gratitude, you can open yourself up to new emotions and experiences. You will feel as if a weight has been lifted. I liken the aftermath to having room in my mental closet. Again, if you don't get rid of the old clothes, then there is no room to bring in new ones. Do not keep the old emotions, thinking, "These will fit again … someday."

I did this after my divorce. I was done with explanations and with my mind constantly spinning as to why my marriage didn't work out in the end. I didn't get the love I needed; he didn't get the love he needed. I could see it all. Asking him to give what he didn't have in him wasn't going to result in a successful union. I wrote it all down, burned it, released it, and let it go forever. And in that act of grace, I was grateful to be able to clear my mind.

If you don't release it, then you continue to be in a spiral. It will affect your future relationships and quality of life.

LIVE IN GRATITUDE

Ask yourself: What am I grateful for in life? Write it down and really dwell on it. Living inside your gratitude will fill you with hope, joy, and purpose. Gratitude will reframe your whole day and your entire life. It is truly the tipping point to abundance. Forgiveness turns the key, while gratitude opens the door.

Some of us will say that we're only grateful for the big things: our marriage, our kids, our home, our town, our job, or our health. I feel there is so much more to add to the list. I'm grateful to wake up in the morning, swing my feet off the bed, and hit the ground that finds them. I'm grateful for this gorgeous place I call home, with the brilliant sun and stars twinkling at night over the ocean. I'm grateful for breakfast, the kind word of a stranger, and that first cool wind of fall. Through it all, I live within gratitude.

Gratitude frames my day. No matter what is happening in my life, there is so much to be grateful for on a daily basis. Forget your current situation if it's difficult. There are always three or four things to list that fill you with hope. Write them down, but don't burn them, because it's helpful to keep a journal where you focus on what's good.

Even on the most challenging days, I always find things to be grateful for *each and every day*. There's always a lesson to learn. I'm especially glad that all I need to do is change my perspective, which is based on my will and choice.

There is a book that has truly helped me over the years called *The Master Key System* by Charles F. Haanel. It's a landmark key to life, written by a man born in 1866 who achieved success as a businessman and author. Haanel, called "the father of personal development," collected life lessons and published them beginning in 1916. His central concept is that everything in the world we see around us was initiated by the creative energy of thoughts as a powerful catalyst in turning a thought into a reality. And these thoughts can help you realize your dreams. Each lesson comes with a meditation at the end.

My copy of Haanel's book has been read many times, as is evidenced by the frayed and marked pages. It's an old friend, as I hope this book will be for you. It has helped me through the decades of my life, and I go back to it again and again. I'm grateful for these teachings, and they remind me that my thoughts of gratitude are now dictating my life.

There are days when I wake up feeling less than grateful. I am human, and so are you. On those days, I have to rewire my thought process because, if I don't, my entire day will be at the mercy of my faulty thinking. I remain in gratitude.

YOU ARE IN CONTROL OF YOU

We are in control of how we respond to our lives. I believe a lot of us react rather than respond. I've had times when I've reacted in a snap to what was going on around me. Now, I prefer to take the time to mull things over. In some cases, I will say, "This is none of my business. I'm gone." This is a way for me to focus on the good in my life instead of sinking low because my fingers are in too many pies that don't belong to me.

UNAPOLOGETIC:

Attention goes where energy flows. When we fixate on the bad, then our light is dim. But through gratitude, the opposite side of pain is the most amazing thing ever.

I know that I have control over my emotions and thoughts. How I think about anything in my life is the most important thing of all. If I think I never will, then believe me, I never will.

One of my favorite quotes of all time is from Henry Ford, who said, "If you think you will … you will. If you think you can't … you won't." Your brain will teach you the ways that you can. This doesn't mean I don't experience levels of failure or feel trepidation. In spite of those feelings, I go right toward the gratitude to level myself out. If I don't, then I won't achieve. I won't get anywhere. I am responsible for holding myself back or not—and gratitude is my secret weapon.

INTERVIEW YOURSELF

Again, your life is an inside job. You must face yourself, know your values, set your boundaries, and then experience gratitude in your life.

To get to that place of gratitude, I highly recommend journaling and meditation, as you might guess. Both allow you to give yourself some attention when many women put themselves last and never get to the "me" part of life. It's important during both exercises that you ask yourself some key questions. Yes, interview yourself. Ask: Where are these feelings coming from? Who am I right now? Is this how I want to show up? How am I doing as a parent, a mate, a friend, a daughter, or as a person? Am I being kind to myself?

The answers will come through your meditation, journaling, or even when working with a coach or therapist. I tell my coach that I'm grateful in life to be an "igniter." I ignite the match, and life often brings the flame. We've talked more about these concepts, as I find coaching to be a serious game changer for me. It's my way of getting to the next level, and I believe the more we level up, the higher we climb.

One word about a coach or therapist: I see mine once a week. Sometimes, if I have great news, we will jump on an additional Zoom call. It's emboldening to find someone who really sees you, even when you can't see yourself, and who holds the space for you even when you can't find it yourself. I love talking to my coach, who is simply a guide and a mirror. A therapist is someone who walks you through trauma. I prefer a coach at the present time, though I'm always grateful to have outside sources to help me.

WHEN NEGATIVITY SEEPS IN

Let's say you think the world is a shitty place. Everything sucks, and nothing is working. Don't deny those feelings—acknowledge them. You can say them out loud or write them down, but don't allow yourself to stay in that place. Say it; call it out: "I'm just going to feel shitty *for today*."

Let it be. Sleep. And move on.

Try not to stay in that bad place. Gratitude will help you out of it because honestly—and I know this in my heart—the world *doesn't* suck, things are not shitty, and everything will work out. There is always, always, always beauty and joy to be found. When I find it, I will call out the good, write it down, and shout it from the mountaintop.

Doom-and-gloom thinking gets and keeps you depressed. Gratitude lifts you up and helps you soar, no matter what is happening. Each time I find my light, I am grateful.

UNAPOLOGETIC:

During tough times, revert to the simple things you can do in as little as five minutes. Take some deep breaths. Imagine releasing negative thoughts. Take your shoes off. Put your feet on Mother Earth. Rub your palms together. Put on some good music and dance. Bring yourself back to a moment of calm. Write down what you are grateful for in life. It really does work.

In my earlier working years, I became friends with one of my managers. He was older and became somewhat of a father figure, one that I'd longed for my entire life. He told me that whenever I have a really challenging conversation with my boss, I should silently send my boss love and blessings. Wouldn't you know that every time I remembered to use that strategy, it worked! Now I use it all the time. I am a firm believer in Universal Consciousness, so I know the vibes I send out to the Universe come back to me.

Whenever I have a particularly challenging day, I remember what this manager said to me, and as I am driving or walking, I send a silent blessing to all I meet. You might think that's too much, but remember—the more you give, the more you are likely to receive.

UNFILTERED:

Much gathers more.

IN THE END

I challenge you to love yourself—warts, big pores, big foreheads, stretch marks, cellulite, and all. Get that internal love dialogue going before you do anything else. Be committed to loving yourself without restraint and to living within gratitude.

A CONVERSATION WITH YOURSELF

Stop telling yourself:

- The world is a shitty place.

- My life is nothing but stress.

- There is no way out.

Start telling yourself:

- There is good in each day if I look for it.

- I can change my life anytime I choose.

- Life is wonderful. I am grateful.

NOTES
FOR YOUR JOURNEY

CHAPTER FOURTEEN
Just Because

"You never need permission to live unfiltered and unapologetically."
—JUDY MCCUTCHEON

If I had to do life over, I would always follow my dreams, mostly with my heart and a little bit of my head. I would take risks and not live my life based on what I think other people expect of me. I would ask questions—lots and lots of questions. I would always be curious and adventurous.

And one more thing …

I know if I had the chance to do life over again, one thing I would never trade is having my daughters. They're keepers, as they say. I'm so fortunate to have them in my life.

As for the rest of it, I hope none of you reading this book cave in to societal pressures. In the end, you have to do you. Be single. Be married. Work at that place or this place—or join the circus! Just be happy. Be mindful. Be kind. It's all up to you.

In the end, you are the only unhappy one if you don't live your life based on the choices your heart tells you to make. Never trade your happiness for the applause of the world. People are fickle. They can turn on you in an instant.

If you're in a marriage or a personal relationship but your heart is not in it, then get out. Don't rob yourself of years of goodness, happiness, love, and intimacy just to live a lie. Eventually, the heart wants what the heart wants, and it will not be denied. Your heart craves happiness. Get out of the resentment before apathy sets in and you are sleepwalking through your days. If you are in a relationship, heart and soul, cherish it. Be grateful. Put even more love and soul into it. Fill your love cup and watch it run over time and time again.

UNFILTERED:

Love and appreciate yourself so you can love and appreciate your partner, your children, and your life.

Life is short, no matter how long you live it. So, live it out loud, live it out hard, and live it with kindness and love. Oh, and remember to eat great food—lots of it (but not all of it)! Drink good wine—life's too short to drink bad wine. Make your health a priority. Everything else in your life depends upon it. As they say, health is wealth.

Find your circle of friends and let it be diverse—older, younger, fatter, taller, etc. Let your circle be wide enough but not too wide. Always have one person in your circle who could lend you $1,000 instantly if you need it, but don't let that be the only reason they are in your circle. Love deep, love hard, love often. Be kind. Be that friend. The one people call in the middle of the night. Be thoughtful. Be bold. Be brave. Be badass.

Live unfiltered and unapologetically. You will never regret it, I promise.

Have those inspiring, life-affirming, blood-stirring conversations with yourself and with your daughters, nieces, sisters, cousins, aunts, mothers, and all the amazing women in your orbit. Women banding together can and will rule the world.

Stand up, speak up, and stand out. Put your shine on, always, so that other women and girls know they can shine, too.

You are badass in every sense of the word. Be extra. Be all that you are meant to be and then some, remembering always that you are everything you need. Celebrate you. I know that I do.

I love and appreciate you.

In gratitude always,

—Judy

P.S.: I would love to hear how you are living unfiltered! Please drop me a note at mccutcheonjudy@gmail.com and follow me on my website www.judymccutcheon.com.

NOTES
FOR YOUR JOURNEY

ACKNOWLEDGMENTS

Writing this book has been a journey of love, reflection, and growth—one I couldn't have completed without my incredible support system. To John, my husband, whose support made this book possible, you've given me the freedom to pursue my dreams while keeping me grounded. To my mother, you taught me what being a badass truly means, and to my daughters, you inspire me to be the woman I needed to see when I was younger.

To the Forbes Books team, thank you for believing in this message and helping to shape it. Special thanks to Cindy—your friendship and guidance throughout this process have been invaluable.

And to everyone who's been part of my journey—thank you for helping me become the unfiltered, unapologetic woman I am today.

www.ingramcontent.com/pod-product-compliance
Lightning Source LLC
Chambersburg PA
CBHW022131080426
42734CB00006B/313